CW00571946

Recipes for Disaster

By the same author:

Laws and Disorders:
A Law-Breaking Guide to Real but Bizarre Laws
from Over the Centuries

French Letters & English Overcoats:
Sexual Fallacies and Fads from Ancient Greece
to the Millennium

Pull the Other One:
Amazing Real Life Excuses from Around the World

Recipes for Disaster

A Deliciously Funny Feast
of True Culinary Catastrophes

By Richard De'ath

Robson Books

First published in Great Britain in 2001 by Robson Books,
10 Blenheim Court, Brewery Road, London N7 9NY

A member of the Chrysalis Group plc

British Library Cataloguing in Publication Data

A catalogue record for this title is available from the British Library

ISBN 1 86105 4696

Typeset by SX Composing DTP, Rayleigh, Essex
Printed by Mackays of Chatham Kent

'Tell the cook of this restaurant with my compliments that these are the very worst sandwiches in the whole world, and that, when I ask for a watercress sandwich, I do not mean a loaf with a field in the middle of it.'

OSCAR WILDE

Acknowledgements:

The author would like to thank the following for their contributions to this feast of fun: Jonathan Waring, Bill Latimer, Alan Watts, John Kent and Keith Larkman. Also the culinary-minded folk at the London Library, the British Museum Newspaper Library at Colindale and the Library of Congress in Washington DC for helping in the search for nourishing morsels. There are also certain others who would rather keep their peculiar tastes to themselves, but to whom I am none the less grateful. All the illustrations are courtesy of *Punch* magazine or my own not-so-tasteful archives.

1

Eat, Drink and Be Wary

There is a classic satirical poem written in the fourteenth century that describes a gourmet's heaven. It's a place where people don't have to sweat and slave to get fed – in fact anyone who sleeps until midday is paid for their repose – and where the buildings are made of fish (salmon, bass and shad) with roofs of bacon and sausages. Lip-smacking meals turn up ready-cooked: geese, for example, roast themselves in the surrounding countryside before flying in, squawking, 'Geese all hot' – bringing with them a little garlic sauce for flavour. Vegetables grow prepared for the table and in the middle of the community is a huge tree which has roots of ginger, bark of cinnamon, boughs of sandalwood, leaves of mace and fruit of cloves. Just to round things off, three times a week it rains 'a deluge of hot tarts'.

No one knows who wrote this description of a hungry man's dream or a sluggard's paradise – depending on your point of view – but it certainly caught the imagination of successive generations, and the famous Flemish painter, Pieter Brueghel, immortalised it in a comic picture of a well-fed group of people dozing amidst the remains of the ultimate, easy-to-make, fast-food lunch. As to the location, it's referred to as *The Land of Cockaigne*. This is not, however, a medieval misprint, but probably a corruption, deliberate or otherwise, from old French *cocaigne*, and the Middle Low German *Kokenje* (small cake). To readers of the time, though, the poem was a sly dig at the luxurious lifestyle of the clergy and the nobility, and the epithet which tripped most easily from hungry mouths when talking about the place was 'The Land of Cockup'.

Today, of course, most people in the West are not faced with the fear of poverty and want which was an ever-present threat in the Middle Ages. In fact, it's been estimated that the average person in the Western world will consume up to seventy tons of food during a lifetime. This all adds up to an awful lot of cooking – whether at home or eating out – and a whole basinful of recipes. Each generation, of course, has its own particular likes and dislikes: chefs of the time pushing the boundaries of cuisine ever further. What they have thrown up (not always literally) has made the history of food endlessly fascinating and often amusing. And while the comedy may not be as direct as in *The Land of Cockaigne*, it can also emerge in a turn of phrase such as Shakespeare's classic line in *Pericles*: 'Come, Gentlemen, we sit too long on trifles.'

The great bard didn't mean the wobbly desserts, naturally. But his is an early example of the *double entendre* and amusing misprint that has bedevilled cookbooks and recipes for centuries. (Shakespeare's obsession with afters didn't quite end there, either, for in *King Lear* appears another memorable line: *Out vile jelly!*) Once started, though, this trend has never ceased. Today, with the ever-increasing number of newspaper and magazine pages devoted to the culinary arts and books of recipes dominating the best-seller lists, it is no surprise that errors still creep in. On television and radio, too, the celebrity chefs have from time to time also been left with egg on their faces after culinary clangers like the nervous Scottish restaurateur who boobed while discussing unexpected guests. 'When vegetarians turnip for dinner they can throw a carrot in the shoup.'

In the pages which follow you will find some of the most amusing gastronomic gaffes that have occurred in

3

restaurants, hotels, everyday kitchens and the various forms of media from all over the world. True stories, I hasten to add, that involve the famous and the not-so-famous, the experienced and the inept, the gourmet and the glutton. All reinforce the statement that it's a good idea to eat, drink and be wary. Let me tempt you with a few *hors d'oeuvres*.

Take some well-known people to begin with. In April 2000, the British Prime Minister, Tony Blair, was interviewed about his cookery skills by *New Woman* and declared, 'I cook a lot of things badly – it's the only thing I can't lie about.' The remark predictably caused smirks among newspaper columnists, but perhaps not quite as many laughs as when American ex-President Bill Clinton was in his first term at the White House, according to a story in the *New Yorker* in May 2000. Discussing menus one day with his chef, Alice Waters, she told him, 'Mr President, catering for you is an excruciating pleasure,' to which he replied, 'You know, that sounds a lot like my job.' Neither reply, though, matches the comment of Joseph Estrada, then Vice-President of the Philippines, a man notorious for his mangled syntax. A report in *The Australian* of August 1996, says he was eating with friends in a restaurant and after failing to catch the eye of a waitress, called the manager and complained: 'I have been fingering your waitress for a long time, but she does not want to come.'

Sex and food are, of course, inextricably linked. To some people, sex is only a substitute for food, as food writer, Liz Leigh, pungently acknowledged not long ago: 'Any man's sexual fervour would come to grief after a six-course meal.' Perhaps the best way of having your cake and eating it is to devour curry – because a report from Nottingham Trent University has argued that curry fans are enjoying much more than korma, tikka masala and rogan josh when they tuck into any Indian dish. It can be as addictive as sex, a research team led by Professor Stephen Gray reported to *The Times* in October 2000: 'It is like sex on a plate. Eating curry gives you a natural "high" much more powerful than anything you get with traditional British foods.'

Although glutton between the covers may not be the ultimate aim of all those visiting restaurants – Indian or otherwise – they have been the setting for a great many culinary catastrophes. It was the French, of course, who invented the restaurant in Paris in the 1760s where they served little cups of meat extract recommended for invalids and those of a nervous disposition. Ostensibly they were health centres and the early ones were to be found listed in trade directories alongside the makers of laxatives and anti-venereal disease pills! The restaurant remained an almost exclusively Gallic phenomenon until the middle of the eighteenth century, when the concept of eating out caught on across Europe. A great French writer, Edmond de Goncourt, who wrote about Parisian society and founded the academy bearing his name which awards annual prizes for fiction, was responsible for upsetting a few delicate stomachs after a night in one of the city's restaurants: 'Very tasty dinner, including some grouse whose scented flesh Daudet compared to an old courtesan's flesh marinated in a bidet.' This said, Goncourt's remarks are merely a forerunner to far worse, like those of journalist Jonathan Cartwright after he had eaten at the Nha Hang Bia Hoi restaurant in Hanoi in 1995. He described his consumer's nightmare in a report for the *Far Eastern Economic Review*:

When the waiter brought me the menu, it included unripe corn-cob soup, fried flour-coated frog and fricasseed bull genitalia. Among the *amuse bouche* were very unamusing salted crickets, small packets of dung beetles and giant red ants' eggs in a salad. Dog came in two styles, kebabed and steamed, and veal came in four styles – kindled, burned, badly burned with raw lemon leaf and burned with burned rice flour. But the *pièce de résistance* was undoubtedly the *not born yet dead cow baby* – stir fried. A Western journalist at another table passed out when she read that.

If you find that unpalatable, then consider the customers of a poultry-dealer in Ghana. When stocks ran out in February 2001, he looked for a solution – and it landed him in jail according to a report in *The Times*. He was charged with killing vultures and selling the plucked birds as chickens. Almost as hard to swallow is the story of Henry Hendrick who was brought before a Polish court in the summer of 1979. His crime? He forced his wife at gunpoint to eat a loud tie she had given him as a birthday present. Misprints, too, can make dishes seem equally as unpalatable, as readers of the *Radio Times*' cookery pages discovered in January 2001: *Cook the carrots, turnips and baby and spring onions individually in boiling, salted water.* While such an error is unlikely to kill anyone, it does point up the fact that cooking can be a dangerous business. Only a few months ago, an American survey revealed that the sixth commonest cause of death is choking on food. And it's as well to be careful with cooking equipment, especially the oven, as 84-year-old Tom Customer found out in February 1982. The Scottish pensioner told a reporter from the *Daily Record*: 'Tuesday was a bad day for me. I had placed my pension and rent books in the oven for safekeeping, but I forgot to take them out while I

6

cooked my lunch and they turned to ash.'

As is so often the case, it is not difficult to find someone worse off. A well-known American story describes the besotted owner of a poodle who washed her pet and then, in a hurry to dry the dog, decided to put it in the microwave for a few moments. She did – and the dog exploded. Around the same time, a British housewife reported that her oven was also being used as a dryer. Mrs Valerie Hart of West Drayton explained in a letter to the *Daily Telegraph*: 'My husband is a keen angler and likes to keep tins of gentles handy in the refrigerator. This is bad enough, but when the cold has made them lethargic he warms them up under the grill, and nothing annoys me more than finding a few stray maggots under the grill when I am about to make the toast for breakfast.' The letter prompted quite a bit of correspondence to the editor, with probably the best reply coming from a retired solicitor in Surrey who wrote: 'Every morning for more than 30 years my wife warmed my bowler hat over the gas ring before I set out for business.'

It's not difficult, when coming across misprints, mistakes, catastrophes and crises, to appreciate why cooking is counted among the most stressful of activities – especially when friends are invited for lunch or when holding a dinner party. Indeed, a Gallup survey in America in November 1996 discovered that holding a dinner party rated on the stress scale to *having mother-in-law over for the weekend*. So if you want a little light relief before your next 'at home' or night out, this book will show that whatever mess you've made of a recipe, whatever problem you've encountered at a restaurant, and to whatever lengths cooking has driven you – someone has been there, done that and got the apron to prove it.

Finally – and to borrow a phrase from the actor and

restaurateur Michael Caine – not many people know this: but it takes one calorie of energy to read a page of 650 words. That's roughly the same amount of energy as you get from eating a tomato or drinking a cup of black coffee. So before we lift the lid off the food world, roast some cookery-book writers and celebrity chefs, and reveal a lot of unsavoury behaviour – perhaps a light snack is called for? Whatever you choose, remember to keep the indigestion tablets handy and in the words of P.G. Wodehouse's man-about-town, Catsmeat Potter-Pirbight: 'May you all have a binge to stagger humanity.'

2

Half-Baked Ideas

It is a well-known fact that many great culinary creations have been born out of disaster. A good example of this is that tasty potato dish *pommes souffles* which came into being thanks to an old chestnut: a late train. In 1863, a French chef, preparing a banquet to mark the opening of a new railway line, had to swiftly change plans when he was told the train was running behind schedule. However, no sooner had he taken his *pommes frites* out of their oil, than news reached him there had been an error in communications and the excursion was actually going to be on time. In exasperation, the chef tipped the half-cooked chips back into the oil – and then watched in amazement as they turned into brown, crispy ovals. Having conjured up a delicacy from the jaws of disaster, the man enjoyed the compliments his new dish received from the assembled diners, explaining with a shrug of his shoulders:

'But, messieurs, they were only *pommes souffles*.'

Of course, mistakes of this kind more often than not turn out to be the curse of a cook's life – especially when they are made in cookbooks and newspaper columns. In this chapter are a selection of misprints from the printed page that could turn any half-baked idea into a soggy surprise, extracted from two thousand years of culinary clangers. For starters, though, where better than a cookery page from the misprint-prone *Grauniad* (aka the *Guardian*) in September 1972:

When next you have friends to dinner, one cut up in a mixed salad would be plenty for eight and a novel surprise for one's guests.

The Carnivore's Banana

One of the very earliest comedies ever written was about food – *The Sausage* cooked up around 500 BC by the Greek dramatist, Epicharmus. Sadly, only fragments of it remain, but they have inspired some classic sausage tales. There is the ancient French tongue twister about Madame de Sanssouci's *six saucisses* costing *six sous*, and a famous German story about the butcher who specialised in sea-bird sausages and while on the beach each day throwing stones at the birds would shout as he hit one, 'There's another tern for the wurst!' In Britain, a government announcement in the austerity-bound days of 1951 that milk powder could be used to improve the protein content of sausages, provoked a question in Parliament: 'How much milk powder can be used in a sausage before it becomes a cream bun?' The Australians have a euphemism for sex, *Hiding the Sos*; an American rap singer recently recorded *Banger!* under the pseudonym MC Banger; and the English entertainer Richard Stilgoe likes to refer to the meaty delicacy as *The Carnivore's Banana*. But one ditty that would surely have best pleased Epicharmus was sung by a lady contestant in the March 1992 British Sausage Song Contest, who, according to an account in the *Daily Telegraph*, trilled:

And when I think of the moment our loving has to end,
A juicy sausage will be my best friend.

A Blow For Seasoning

Titus Maccius Plautus was known as the chief comic poet of Rome around 180 BC – although he had struggled for years to get anyone to perform his plays. For a time he even worked for a miller turning a hand-mill while scribbling out his satirical comedies of everyday life. Yet despite years of poverty, Plautus developed a passion for good food and in one of his plays, *Menaechmi*, made some pungent remarks about cooks. A later English mistranslation of the book would undoubtedly have tickled his palate:

> *When these chaps season the dinners that they cook, they use for seasoning no seasonings, but screech-owls, to eat the entrails out of living guests. This explains why people here have such short lives – filling their bellies full of fodder of this sort, ghastly to mention, let alone to eat. Why, those that fart on food that I have seasoned are enabled to live as much as 200 years.*

Cocky Leeks

Some of the earliest recipes are to be found in the record books of the medieval English Court. Among these are such tasty dishes as *Pokerounce*, *Rapeye*, *Tart on Ember Day* and *Slit Slops* which consists of leeks, brown bread, oil and a glass of wine. To make a portion for four persons, *A*

Proper Newe Book of Cookerye, published in 1545, instructed cooks:

> *Take a good leek and trim bottom before simmering for 15 minutes, covering the pan.*

Never On A Full Stomach

Probably the most important cookery book of the Renaissance was *Ein New Kochbuch* by the German Max Rumpolt. Published in 1604 with many woodcuts, its long title page promised readers instructions on how to cook just about everything, including a huge number of birds and animals and even a wild horse! Translations of the *Kochbuch* into English suffered any number of misplaced c's and f's – especially in Rumpolt's delightful recipes for duck. Rumpolt also cautioned against combining eating and sex, following the lead of Andrew Borde, an Englishman whose name belied his concerns. In his *Compendyous Regyment; or, a Dyetary of Health* (1542) Borde warned:

> *Beware of veneryous acts before the first sleep, and specially beware of such things after dinner or after a full stomach, for it doth engender the crap and the gout and other displeasures.*

Tickling The Queen's Fancy

The Queen's Closet Opened which appeared in 1645 was claimed to be the recipes and household advice of Henrietta Maria, the consort of Charles I. Despite its title, the book is believed to have been written by a man with a taste for suggestive humour as these lines from the first edition suggest:

> *This decockion is good to eate both before and after meate for it will make digestion good and turn your meate to pure blood. Beside all this it doth excell, all windiness to expell.*

The Pigskin Special

The anonymous author of *A Garland of Dishes* published in the seventeenth century was probably none too pleased to find that the printer had managed to make a mockery of one of his favourite recipes in the first edition:

> *To make a piece of boiled bacon the better in flavour, add to the water a little vinegar, a small piece of nutmeg, and a couple of gloves.*

Half-Baked – 1

Victorian writers and philosophers were great ones for getting it wrong – not least when writing about food. Take this half-baked idea from John Herschel's *A Preliminary Discourse on the Study of Natural Philosophy* published in 1830:

Who, for instance, would have conceived that sawdust is susceptible of conversion into a substance bearing no remote analogy to bread? Though certainly less palatable than that of flour, yet no way disagreeable, and both wholesome and digestible as well as highly nutritative? This discovery, which renders famine next to impossible, deserves a higher degree of celebrity than it has obtained.

Half-Baked – 2

Another man not lost for the wrong words who signed himself T. Baron Russell was even more emphatic in his little treatise, *A Hundred Years Hence* issued in 1905:

Such a wasteful food as animal flesh cannot survive: and even apart from the moral necessity which will compel mankind, for its own preservation, to abandon the use of alcohol, the direct and indirect wastefulness of alcohol will make it impossible for beverages containing it to be tolerated. Very likely tobacco will follow it.

Half-Baked – 3

Half a century later, a Mr S.K. Spokes was urging that people in the East should not be encouraged to eat beef as it engendered violence. He was quoted in the *Leicester Mercury* in April 1960:

My experience is that to give men plenty of red meat to eat makes them so fit that they become almost violent. I think we have enough trouble with the violent people we already have, and I suggest we leave these people to their rice. Let us not aggravate the situation by wanting them to start eating beef.

A Royal Cock-Up

Queen Victoria would doubtless not have been amused if she had turned to a recipe for chicken in the pages of *A Plain Cookery Book for the Working Classes* written by one of her chefs, Charles Elme Francatelli, and published in 1848. Francatelli, a former *maitre d'hotel* and one of the first writers to try to introduce the art of cooking to ordinary housewives, was not helped in his cause by this misprint:

I hope that at some time you may afford yourself an old hen or cock, and when this occurs, this is the way in which I recommend that it be cooked: viz – First fuck, draw, singe off the hairs, and then tie the bird up in a plump shape.

Handy Instructions

Another campaigner for better eating among the Victorian poor was Edward Ballard, a physician at the Farringdon General Hospital in London, who in 1854 wrote a little tome, *On Pain After Food: It's Cause & Treatment*. In a chapter on the 'Evil Results of Hurried Meals' Ballard compared those who ate too quickly as being 'like the insane in the way they devour the food placed before them' and warned his lady readers of the effects this could have on their husbands:

> *The principal meal of the day, in place of being leisurely taken and enjoyed, is too often snatched at some uncertain hour, casually furnished by a brief interval of business. A few minutes only, and possibly these interruptedly, being perhaps allotted with impatient and niggard hand, to the ceaseless toil. This hasty dispatch not only interferes with the due process of masturbation, but also with the secretion of the juices which flow in obedience to sapid impressions into the mouth.*

Cooking The Books

The first superstar of the recipe book was Isabella Beeton whose *Household Management* was originally issued in instalments in 1859–60. It made her a household name, and some of her phrases like 'A place for everything and everything in its place' have remained familiar ever since. Another of her nostrums insisted, 'There is no more fruitful source of family discontent than a housewife's badly cooked dinners and untidy ways.' One thing she *didn't* say, though it is now part of the folklore of cookery, is 'First, catch your hare.' Some experts, however, believe that Mrs Beeton was a bit of a fraud and couldn't cook and probably never tested her recipes. She has even been blamed for watery, over-cooked English vegetables. What Mrs B cannot be blamed for, though, was this misprint in the first instalment of her *magnum opus*:

It is not considered polite to tear bits off your beard and put them in your soup.

The Female Touch

An American chef, Felix J. Deliee, was a master of the lightest delicacies, but fell victim to the heavy hand of the printer's devil in his *Franco-American Cookery Book; or, How To Live Well and Wisely Every Day of the Year* (1884). Deliee, who was then the caterer at the prestigious New

York Club, offered his readers this recipe for *LADY FINGERS*:

Cover partially with the preparation and bake until firm and of a slight brown colour. Allow them to cool perpendicularly to prevent them getting moist when cocking.

Dressed To Thrill

One of Mrs Beeton's earliest rivals was the American, Harriet De Salis, author of a popular series of *A La Mode* cookery books dealing with entrees, savouries and other courses published on both sides of the Atlantic in the 1880s. Mrs De Salis, who lived in New York, described herself in the introduction to *Dressed Vegetables A La Mode* (1888) as 'devoted to hunting in the happy grounds of cooking' and offered this mangled recipe for *Asparagus a la Tod Heatley*:

Cook the asparagus as usual, then lay on ice or in a refrigerator. When properly cold, arrange bunches like faggots and garnish with whipped aspic. This dish is also very good with simply a green mayonnaise over it.

The Demon Drink

Quite a few Victorian cookbooks were keen on warning their readers against the evils of drink. One such volume was *The Demon of Dyspepsia; or, Digestion Perfect &* *Imperfect* published by Adolphus E. Bridger in 1888. Bridger, a London doctor, a Fellow of the Therapeutical Society of Great Britain, and the author of *Biliousness* (1886), delivered this message:

> *Alcohol, in any shape and form, is best omitted from the dietary of women till they are at least fifty years of age. If their temperament be at all emotional it should, prior to that period, be most strictly forbidden.*

One In The Oven

Men came in for some equally strong words from the author of *The Aladdin Oven: What It Is – What It Does – How It Does It*. Written in 1892 by an American physician, Doctor Edward Atkinson, he told his readers that he had made a thorough study of the oven and warned:

> *I believe men have no right to scold their wives, or use swear words about the cook, and find fault with their meals in a constant and promiscuous way, if they only supply them with apparatus to cook with that is not fit to be used . . . The way out of this dilemma is for every boy to be put in the way of learning how to make first-rate bread and buns in the oven.*

Butter Pats

Anne Wallbank Buckland, a distinguished member of the Anthropological Institute in London, compiled a weighty tome full of exotic titbits about the history of food in 1893. The book, *Our Viands: Whence They Came and How They Are Cooked*, contained this amusing paragraph:

> *The most ancient butter of which we have any real knowledge is that known as Bog Butter which is dug up from time to time in Irish peat-bogs. Two or three nobs of this butter may be seen in the Museum of the Royal Irish Academy in Dublin.*

The English Delicacy

Madame Marie de Joncourt was a rival of Mrs Beeton but fared rather worse than her at the hands of proof-readers. Two errors in the worst possible taste appeared in the first edition of her *Wholesome Cookery* (1895). The recipe for Buff Pudding became *Muff Pudding* which added a saucy flavour to her comment that it was, 'Good warm, but better hot.' A section dealing with cakes caused her even more embarrassment:

> *In modern times, the bum appears to have become an almost exclusively English delicacy, and in the last century there were special houses to which the elite resorted to enjoy*

*them. Two of these are historically famous: the Chelsea
and its rival the Royal.*

Fanny's Favourites

America's first famous cookery expert, Fannie Farmer,
'the mother of level measurement', actually had to pay for
her work, *The Boston Cooking-School Cook Book,* to be
published in 1896. Its success, though, was such that it
later made her millions of dollars and changed the cooking
habits of American women for ever. Among the unusual
recipes to be found in the book's pages were *Ambushed
Asparagus, Cape Cod Berry Grunt, Dorothy Dimple's Vinegar
Candy* and *A Nun's Sigh* which appeared in the first
edition with this error.

These souffles – *as light as a nun's sigh – are made of
chou paste, the base for cream poofs and eclairs.*

Bully For Breakfast

A London housekeeper, Mrs M.L. Allen, set herself up as a one-woman campaigner to improve the British breakfast in the closing years of the Victorian era. She wrote her book, *Breakfast Dishes For Every Morning of the Month* in 1896 'because almost everyone complains of the monotony of breakfast dishes, which consist for the most part of boiled eggs, bacon, sausages or dried fish'. Among her recipes for a change were:

Curried Bollock's Sweetbreads.

Blue For Danger

Chicago chef, Maximilian De Loup, was noted for his novel way with salads. In 1901 he wrote *The American Salad Book*, claimed to be 'the most complete, original and useful collection of salad recipes ever brought together' – though who would have fancied this particular suggestion by De Loup is surely a matter of taste:

For a violent lunch or dinner, a salad can be made of the blue violet so common throughout the Northern States.

The Wind Of Change

The Belly Book; or, Diner's Guide by the French dietician and Doctor of Literature, C. Louis Leipoldt, was an eclectic helping of strange facts about food and cooking collected from all over the world and intended to encourage culinary experimentation. Published in 1911, it described how nearly every variety of animal had been used somewhere in the world to provide meat for the table – including llama cutlets (South America) and elephant's foot (in Venice, of all places). In Constantinople, said the author, 'fashionable men and women enjoy excellent bare steaks'. A more amusing paragraph still awaited later in the book:

> *Cardinal du Prat, who was renowned for the excellence of his diners, believed in heating ingredients to boiling point and then allowing them to simmer, especially in the preparation of spinach. Vegetables treated in this fashion, usually with the addition of farts, are excellent.*

The Art Of Handling

The early years of the twentieth century saw an ever-increasing number of cookery books being published, a number written by housewives as well as all the chefs and cooks. Mrs W. Phipson Beale was typical of these, claiming that her *Letters To Young Housewives* (1912) had been distilled from the expertise of friends 'and their experienced housekeepers'. Though what any of them made of the following misprinted statement can only be imagined:

There is one thing the young mistress of the present day does not appear to grasp and that is that the management of the household cocking requires perseverance, judgement and the art of calculating carefully the proportion.

Testament To The Sauce

Cooks often make notes in recipe books – but none stranger than that found in a volume belonging to Maggie North of Philadelphia in 1913. According to the report of her death in the *Philadelphia Daily News* she had used the recipe for 'Chili Sauce Without Working' for her *will*:

Chop tomatoes, onions and peppers fine, add the rest mixed together and bottle cold. Measure tomatoes when peeled. In case I die before my husband I leave everything to him.

Sandwich Spread

Prompted by what he described as 'the vogue of the sandwich now developing from a fashionable craze into a permanent institution', a London cook, M. Redington

White wrote *Something New in Sandwiches* in 1932. This included dozens of recipes for sandwiches, many of which were years ahead of the exotic fillings now to be found in snack bars all over the world. Among the section on 'Hot Sandwiches' appeared the 'Atta-Boy':

> *Cut the corn from the required number of green corn nobs and cook it in slightly salted water for half an hour until it becomes thick and pulpy.*

Stirring Verse

Monica Dickens, the great-granddaughter of Charles Dickens, who became famous for her book, *One Pair of Hands*, in 1939, had planned her first work to be a cookery book in verse. Although she was deterred from this idea by her publisher, Michael Joseph, who fancied an auto-biography from the young debutante, a verse from the original still survives:

> *If the grains of rice could talk,*
> *They'd clamour, 'Stir us with a fork'.*

Stuff Of Delight

With a title like *Cunning Cooking* (1939), the historian Geoffrey Boumphrey was surely inviting trouble from the printer's devil. In a section dealing with fillets of meat and fish, the first edition of the book contained this paragraph:

Fillets should be rolled around an interesting filling and the thread with which each is tied must be removed before serving. Stuffed fillies should be firm-fleshed.

Kept In Store

In March 1940, with the Second World War at the doorstep of Britain's kitchens, the *Daily Telegraph* reported that a series of lectures about the conservation of food were to be delivered at the Royal Institute in London during the months of April, May and June. The Minister of Food, Lord Wootton, was scheduled to give a speech at the meetings which were to be called:

The Nation's Larder and the Housewife's Part Therein.

Trading Places

The Lady magazine was a repository of information for housewives and mothers throughout the war years with page after page of recipes and culinary tips. In the spring of 1941, the editor's column noted, 'This is the time of year when the heart of the housewife turns to marmalade.' But more amusing was a small advert placed the following year:

LADY will exchange clothing, self, little girl, for farm butter, eggs, jam.

Parsley Sauce

Another popular journal for the ladies, *Woman's Own*, did its best to keep readers' spirits high by encouraging them to carry on social engagements as normal. Dinner parties should still be held, it urged, and in November 1941 suggested:

With any of these dainty decorations you can prepare unusual dishes and show your guests your originality without having to fall back on little bunches of parsley.

The magazine's fascination with parsley cropped up again in another painful predicament:

Save time and cut fingers with a parsley mincer.

Heavy Meal

A rival publication, *Women's Realm,* was also bedevilled by its printer in an issue devoted to making the most of rationed foods. Staff writer Margaret Hepworth in a column of handy tips stated:

For coping with unexpected guests, it is always a good plan to keep a few tons of sardines in the house.

A Hitch In Time

Throughout the Second World War, the Ministry of Food issued a number of pamphlets of recipes entitled *The Kitchen Front* which utilised such food as was available to the cooks of Britain. No doubt householders licked their lips at the thought of 'Beetroot Soup', 'Oatmeal Sausages', 'Sugarless Sweets' and 'Eggless Cake'. There was also a concerted campaign to make everyone eat more carrots which, it was said, 'Keep you healthy and help you see in the Blackout.' The RAF also claimed its pilots were on a daily diet of carrots which enabled them to see at night and *this* was why they were giving the Nazi airmen such a pasting. In fact, it was to fool the Germans about the invention of Radar, the real reason for the successes. The pamphlets were often produced hastily and under difficult conditions in war-torn London, which meant that misprints occurred regularly. These typical examples appeared in leaflets distributed between 1940–43:

> * *Mix thoroughly and make sure the mixture is fairly stiff.*
> *It is best to take off the cloth before eating . . .*
> * *Serve on a bed of vice . . .*
> * *If you follow the instructions carefully, these recipes can*
> *be successfully achieved without a bitch . . .*

Pet Problems

The Ministry of Food issued countless announcements to food manufacturers. This classic bit of bureaucratic gobbledegook was dated 20 August 1941:

> *A new licence has been issued authorizing the use of*
> *manufacture of food for animals of any Wheat by-product*
> *and also of any milled Wheaten substance produced from*
> *unmillable wheat. Millers should note that for the purpose*
> *of this Licence, 'animals' includes birds, but not cats or*
> *dogs.*

What Is A Cook?

The hand of the bureaucrat was also evident in a leaflet issued to the catering industry in 1944 by the Industrial and Staff Canteen Undertakings Wages Board. Under Paragraph 9 of the Wages Regulations Proposals ran the sentence:

A cook is a male or female worker of 21 years of age or over wholly or mainly engaged in the preparing and cooking of food requiring the mixing of two or more ingredients with, or without, assistance.

The War Effort

Doctor N. Gangulee, an expert on nutrition, added his weight to the war effort in Britain with a book, *What To Eat and Why*, published in 1944. The good doctor was concerned about keeping the nation 'regular' amid the strain of war and urged his readers:

You must guard yourself against faulty elimination of waste products. Imperfect action of the bowels or constipation is very injurious to health, but it can be easily corrected if you are wise in choosing the right foods. Figs, dates, prunes, mangoes, apples, cucumber and all crapped vegetables are good laxative foods.

Rolling On

Things were not much better for Britons in the days of austerity which followed the end of the war. At least the cookery pages in the press tried to be more inspiring – if unintentionally humorous – as this example for 'Cheap Sponge Roll' in the *Bristol Times & Mirror* of August 1946 demonstrates:

Take a teacupful of flour and mix it with a teacupful of caster sugar and a teaspoonful of baking powder. Break two eggs into a cup, then slide into the mixture.

Chipped Portions

The return of plentiful fish and chips was welcomed throughout Britain – especially in the North where they had been one of the staple dishes for years. A feature article about this good news appeared in the *Liverpool Echo* in December 1946 containing this titbit of information:

Some people do not know that they can be treated exactly like chipped potatoes, that is cut in thin slice and friend in deep fat.

Class Potatoes

Potatoes were claimed to be a sign of social standing in an article in the *Daily Express* in July 1944. The unsigned piece on the cookery page declared:

If you eat salad for lunch or dinner you are probably upper-class. Raw tomato and carrots are the mark of a high social class. But serve potatoes only without vegetables and your lower-class origins are showing.

Ring Of Confidence

Sometimes newspapers and magazines own up to their clangers. The weekly paper, *Reveille*, had fun at its own expense in February 1947:

Owing to a printer's error in the 'Fairy-Ring' cake recipe last week, 'two ounces of caster oil' was given for 'two ounces of caster sugar'. We apologise for this silly mistake.

Skinned Dipping

The American press was no better at this time in its cookery pages. The prestigious *Boston Globe* was as flushed with embarrassment as its subject – beetroots – when this recipe slipped into print in May 1949:

Wash beets very clean, then boil. When done, swim out into a pan of cold water and slip the skins off with the fingers.

A Slippery Problem

During a campaign to encourage greater cleanliness in the kitchen, the *Seattle Post Intelligence* of March 1950 offered this piece of advice:

After removing the meat from your broiling pan allow it to soak in soapy water.

Chicken Surprise

Judy Miller, the cookery writer of the *Ridgewood Record* in New Jersey, loved chicken dishes and regularly provided her readers with new ideas. In November 1951, many got a chuckle from this slip of the typewriter:

Order chicken cut into serving pieces. Clean as necessary. Wash, drain, and blot on absorbent paper. Place chicken in deep bowl. Mash in a mortar the garlic, oregano, salt and peppercorns. Add to rum, mixed with soy sauce. Pour over children.

Scrambled Dish

A daily recipe in the famous *Washington Post* in May 1952 produced a singularly apt printer's error which no doubt amused readers in that seat of government. It was entitled 'Baked Porgies' and read:

4 porgies each weighing ³⁄₄ to 1 lb.
1 lemon cut in four slices
1 teaspoon salt
1 tablespoon chopped archives

34

A Little Learning

A printer's gremlin got the equally distinguished *New York Times* into a similar spot of culinary bother later that same year. A daily column of quick tips for readers in October 1952 suggested:

Just for a change of pace, serve diced cooked carrots and peas in a cheese sauce to which a little finely grated opinion has been added.

Egg Flop

Another famous American newspaper, the *Chicago Sun-Times* added to the great blooper tradition shortly afterwards in a column devoted to the different ways of preparing coffee. An issue in June 1953 stated:

Gourmets will be interested in an instant coffee with egg, bottled garlic and preserved onion rings.

Tea's Up!

Britain's *Sunday Mirror* gave over a page in an issue of November 1953 to the qualities of tea. The paper's consultant GP, Dr Bloomfield, was especially keen on the restorative powers of a cuppa at the start of the day:

That early morning (not too early!) cup of tea, daintily served with a biscuit or two, will work wonders in getting folk up in time for breakfast the following morning.

Passion Killer

The syndicated column of cookery hints in the *Romford Recorder* written by Lilly Matthews, an American cookery expert who had settled in the country after the war, was popular for its recipes using fresh fruits. Poor Miss Matthews dropped a real peach when she wrote in August 1953:

To serve, dip moulds in water to loosen the contents and serve with passion fruit and cream. British housewives can substitute pineapples, cherries or apricots for passion.

Relative Values

The hot summers in the south of America have prompted cookery writers to stress the importance of preserving food carefully during these months. A special section in the *Albany Journal* in July 1955 contained this comic misprint:

Keeping all food under cover is the first step towards ridding the house of aunts.

36

Bubbling Over

The weekly front-page spot on the *Indianapolis Star* offered readers a recipe every day which was always relevant to the time of year. In the middle of a particularly cold winter in December 1960, the paper decided dumplings were what was required to warm up the chilliest mortal and suggested:

Drop hot cooked rice into hot soap by spoonfuls and you will have rice dumplings.

Pissoles In The Snow

Cold-weather dishes were also featured in a special edition of the *Manchester County Express* in November 1963. The anonymous cook was no doubt desperate to hide his (or her) blushes when the paper came out:

After you have prepared your chips, why not at the same time fry a couple of pissoles while the fat is still hot. Together with some salad, cut-up tomatoes and an egg, you now have a delicious hot lunch.

The Uplifting Of Tripe

As part of a feature in September 1964 to enlighten its readers into the delights of tripe, the long-established *Birmingham Mail* described some of the traditional ways of serving the dish. This paragraph obviously escaped the attention of the proof-reader:

Connoisseurs only place tripe, feet, and condiments by layers in their brassiere, first the carrots, then the tripe and pieces of beef.

The Height Of Fusion!

The editor of the 'Woman's Page' in the *Barrow News* suffered the indignity of a paragraph from her fashion column getting mixed into the daily recipe in an issue in June 1964:

Add the remainder of the milk, beat again, turn quickly into buttered pans and bake half an hour. Have the oven hot, twist a length of narrow green ribbon around them, and you have a pretty bouquet for your dress or hat.

Much the same thing happened on a page for women in the *Guardian* in February 1971. In answer to a question from 'L.G.S.', the editor wrote:

For the delicate lingerie you describe, we think that you will find the water in which a quantity of unsalted rice has been boiled quite sufficient stiffening. Wait until the mixture is cold before adding the flavouring.

Chicken Dip

The Irish magazine, *Women's Way*, runs a popular feature answering questions from readers. In January 1965, the following request appeared from a Dublin housewife:

Please can you suggest a cold fish dish to be made from leftover chicken?

Grilled Ear

Peanut butter has become a popular ingredient in a number of US recipes as the *American Weekly* magazine demonstrated in April 1967. Among those dishes listed was 'Peanut Butter Grilled Corn' which was described in these painful terms:

Husk fresh corn and spread the ears lightly with peanut butter. Wrap each ear with bacon slice and fasten with a toothpick. Place on grill, turning until done – about ten minutes. Or let everyone grill his own ears, using long skewers to do so.

Mincing Words

Most of the first edition of *Caribbean Cooking for Pleasure* by Mary Slater had been sold in 1968 before a reader pointed out a misprint to the publishers:

The same arrangement of cold rice and vegetables can be made with shrimps, lobster or left-over minced cold children instead of eggs.

The Way To A Man's Heart

The popular woman's magazine, *She*, contained a supplement in its September 1969 issue devoted to meals for 'tempting the man in your life'. One writer, Jennifer Young, had this suggestion:

The way to his heart might lie in the tricky art of cooking his liver.

Two decades later, with women's lib in full flower, an unknown graffiti artist offered a rather different suggestion on the walls of King's College, London:

Food is not the way to a man's heart – a wooden stake is.

A Fowl Dish

The Christmas spirit was obviously still alive and well on the *Oxford Star* when it offered readers suggestions for using up left-over items from the festive board. The issue of 27 December 1978 carried not one but two boners in its ideas for turkey:

> *A turkey is now a highly economical bird and can be burned into a number of interesting savoury fishes for the post-Christmas period.*

The Scent Of Swine

The *Guardian* managed to mangle a story about that great delicacy, the truffle, in publishing an article from a Reuters correspondent in its cookery section in September 1979. The piece ran:

> *In France, truffles are often found by pigs, who have a keen nose for the scent of the underground tuber, although swine tend to eat the plant and must be kept away from the truffles after they are traced. In Italy, however, farmers prefer to locate truffles with specially trained gods, who can be of any breed and are often a mixed breed.*

A Tall Order

In common with many other newspapers, the *Manchester Evening News* has run reviews of local restaurants for many years. The paper is particularly good at describing the ingredients of dishes, but after a visit to one establishment in 1980, their exuberant food writer, Frank Wynne, suffered from a touch of printer's error:

Throwing caution to the winds, I ordered a tournedos (well done, with a mixed salad and baked potatoes) and a half giraffe of wine.

Sex And The Single Potato

There was a touch of verbosity in Dr Cyril Daly's article for the *Irish Medical Times* in November 1984. Writing about the importance of the potato in Irish history, he said that because they could grow in the poor quality Irish soil, they had proved a godsend to Irish sexuality and led to the population boom in the late eighteenth century. He added:

Far from being a simple culinary irrelevance, the potato is a passionate and violent tuber carrying within its sightless eyes memories of violence, death and sexuality.

Flushed With Pride

Cookery books produced by women's organisations to raise funds have become increasingly commonplace in recent years. Some have solicited their favourite recipes of film and television personalities, while others have printed their members' most popular dishes. A report of one such publishing venture in the *Essex County Standard* in October 1985 was bedevilled by a comic juxtaposition of facts:

> *The ladies of the County Medical Society Auxiliary plan to publish a Cookbook. Part of the proceeds will go to the Samaritan Hospital to purchase a stomach pump.*

Meat Or Men?

A report in *Book News* of November 1985 described a discussion by a women's group in Brighton on the pros and cons of vegetarianism. One speaker told the audience: 'Eating cut-up dead animals is bad for you, like heterosexuality, and once you realise the fact it is easy to give up both.' To which a response was heard from among the assembled company:

> *Meat and men are probably bad for women, but I want my right not to be perfect.*

Kneading Bread

An article in the *Guardian* on the 'sensual, almost sexy' pleasure to be had from breadmaking by Walter Schwarz in January 1986 prompted several letters to the editor including this one from Tim Burton:

In spite of the incredulity of friends and the embarrassment of my wife, I have for years been extolling the pleasure of kneading bread in the nude. Mr Schwarz's article has vindicated me and will, I hope, lead to a more widespread adoption of this very liberating practice. Believe me, it's the best way to become a master-baker.

A Smalls Matter

The visit by cookery writer Valerie Tedder to the Melton Historical Society in December 1988 was eagerly awaited by its members. Even the local paper, the *Melton Times*, previewed the visit – although the editor had to issue an embarrassed apology in the following week's issue:

Melton Historical Society members heard a talk by Valerie Tedder about her book, The Pantry Under The Stairs, *not* The Panty Under The Stairs *as reported in Club Corner last week.*

Asparagus Tips

Two of Britain's leading contemporary novelists, Ian McEwan and Julian Barnes, have both written of their passion for asparagus. McEwan wrote in *Boulevard* in August 1979:

Eaters of asparagus know the scent it lends the urine. It has been described as reptilian, or as a repulsive inorganic stench, or again as a sharp, womanly odour and exciting. Certainly it suggests sexual activity of some kind between exotic creatures, perhaps from a distant land, another planet. This wordly smell is a matter for poets and I challenge them to face their responsibilities.

Julian Barnes was a little more succinct in his mention in the *New York Review* in December 1989:

If the Mona Lisa ate asparagus, it would show in her urine; and this would make her richer, both as a woman and as a subject for art.

Kiddies' Favourite

Another culinary choker which resulted in a newspaper apology appeared in the *Leamington Spa Observer* in March 1991:

> *The* Observer *wishes to apologise for a typesetting error in our 'Tots and Toddlers' advertising feature last week which led to Binswood Nursery School being described as serving 'children casserole' instead of chicken casserole.*

Making A Pig Of Yourself

A word made all the difference in the advertisement for a new title from the Merton Press which appeared in the *Daily Telegraph* in March 1999:

> *HOW TO EAT WELL AGAIN*
> *On a Wheat, Glutton and Dairy Free Diet*

Comic Capers

The cartoonist Mel Calman and his friend, Adrian Bailey, co-authored one of the most amusing and instructive cookery columns of the eighties, *The Cartoon Cook*, which ran in the *Sunday Mirror* magazine. Calman loved risqué definitions – and this was his favourite:

Coq Au Vin – Sex in the back of a van.

The Problem Of Wind

The *Times* cook, Fiona MacCarthy, devoted a section to baked beans in her column in January 1987 which featured a number of recipes as well as comments from several chefs. MacCarthy referred to one well-known lady chef:

Beans get her going on a learned disquisition on the cultural significance of farting, to which she appends the cook's tip that to stew them with wild chicory lessens the likelihood of a grand explosion.

Frenchman's Fancy

There were embarrassed faces on the staff of the *Blackburn Citizen* in Lancashire in June 1993 when a review of a local restaurant by a staff reporter appeared with this sentence:

Mushrooms Provencale stuffed with the chef's special recipe and friend in a garlic butter.

Pie In The Sky

When a new edition of *Exciting English Dishes* by Rigmore Williams was published in May 1985, the book was widely reviewed. However, the facts about the cuisine in Barlow, North Yorkshire, rather worried Lawrence Shelley, the town's Chief Information Officer. He told the *Yorkshire Post*: 'One does not like to look a gift horse in the mouth, but Mr Williams has got it wrong when he says, "Barlow retains its small shops that specialise in the superb local pies," for there are no pie shops in Barlow.' Asked to comment by the *Post*, the author replied:

Well, I came away with a strong impression of pies.

Use Your Loaf

Surely one of the most unlikely recipes ever appeared in the *Lodz Daily News* in Poland where it was spotted by a reader of *Private Eye* and sent in to that magazine's amusing column, 'True Stories' in February 1986:

BREAD CUTLETS: Soak dry bread and milk. Squeeze. Mince. Re-mince with a chopped onion. Add two eggs, salt, pepper. Mould into cutlets. Fry until brown. Delicious with any kind of sauce.

Breakfast With Mother

The annual *Egon Ronay Guides* have become a valuable source of opinions on restaurants and hotels thanks to the standards of taste set by their founder and chief inspector. In June 1988, Ronay was doing his usual publicity tour for the new edition and met up with a reporter from the *Daily Mail*. The following day the paper carried this story:

> *Egon Ronay is mounting a campaign to bring back the breakfast. I asked if we could meet over the best breakfast he could think of and, naturally, he recommended his mother.*

Mice Is Nice

In April 1990, the Stevenage Animal Rights group issued a pamphlet of recipes in which the ingredients contained no animal meat whatsoever. All except one, that is, where a typo ruined their intentions and resulted in the snack being quoted in a number of newspapers including the *Daily Mail*:

> *CRUELTY FREE SPAGHETTI BOLOGNESE: Stir in 1 teaspoon of yeast extract with a well-minced meat substitute. Chop onions and mushrooms. Fry onions in the margarine (much nicer than oil). Cook till soft. Add mushrooms and the mice, cook for 2 mins. Add everything else and simmer for 10 mins.*

Chew All You Want

The well-known American jet-setting gourmet, Laura Corrigan, surprised a reporter from the *Los Angeles Times* in October 1995 with a classic malapropism while she was discussing her favourite foods. Recently, she said, she had to go and see her doctor because she was suffering from indigestion problems and did not want to lose her appetite. The reporter enquired what he had recommended:

My doctor told me if you want to avoid indigestion, you must masturbate, masturbate, masturbate.

Rinse Thoroughly

And to prove that even the latest computer technology cannot keep the printer's devil out of food, one of the great traditional dishes of England suffered this indignity in the pages of the *North Devon Journal* in January 2001:

Other recipes include past favourites such as jugged hair.

3

Medium Rare

In the autumn of 2000, the brilliant comedienne Maureen Lipman complained, 'Television at the moment, what is it? Gardening with breasts, cooking and lunatics and flies on the wall, so where is the room for anything decent?' Cooking with lunatics might be a bit of a harsh judgement, but there is certainly no shortage of larger-than-life chefs who have brightened up the box with their humour – often deliberately, but occasionally unintentionally. Nor is this something new. The truth is, of course, that it's not only eggs that get broken during the making of radio and television cookery programmes. There's a whole history of gastronomic gaffes to be found in the archives of broadcasting.

Many years ago, one of those haughty-voiced BBC announcers introduced a cookery programme for housewives with the aside that one of the recipes for cooking pigeon, 'fills me with excrement'. On an even more notorious occasion, another poor announcer informed those tuned in to the war-time show, *The Kitchen Front*, that they were listening to the 'British Broadcorping Castration'. In those days, programmes were live and there was no hiding from mistakes. Nowadays, pre-recording shows has meant the clangers and spoonerisms are usually only revealed in programmes of outtakes. But escape they do, because as chef Anthony Bourdain explained in his recent book, *Kitchen Confidential*, 'There's an oral tradition in kitchens of playing with words, telling jokes and insulting one another' which he believes is unavoidable whenever food is being prepared. Which reminds me of another strangled saying attributed to an American announcer in the days of live television: 'We must be careful about getting too many cooks into this soup or somebody's going to think there's dirty work behind the crossroads.' Above all, though, never forget *the* cook's quote which is underlined by every item in this section:

Spice is the variety of life.

Boiling Point

During the Second World War, the voice of cookery expert Ambrose Heath became familiar to millions of British listeners on his early morning radio broadcasts, *Kitchen Front Recipes*. Already well known for his series of *Good Food* books and columns in the *News Chronicle* and *Country Life*, he introduced his audience to such delights as 'Beetroot Buns', 'Green Tomato Jam', 'Flower Fritters', 'Watercress Puree' and various easy ways of cooking nettles. Always exuberant and full of good cheer, encouraging listeners in the embattled nation to 'stoke up' in order to keep healthy, Heath dropped one glorious clanger in December 1940:

When this is done, sit on a very hot stove and stir frequently.

Milk Maidens

Butter was in short supply throughout much of the Second World War in Britain, and food experts were forever offering alternatives in their recipes. The shortage became something of a standing joke, especially through the catch-phrase of Sam Fairfechan, a grocer in the hugely popular radio comedy show, *ITMA*, which starred Tommy Handley. Fairfechan used to greet his customers with the lines, 'We have no butter today, it's all under the counter.' As the war drew to a close, however, butter became a little more readily available and broadcasters like Elizabeth Forster started to give their listeners cooking tips in which it was included. During the hot summer of 1944, Miss Forster advised:

Keep butter and milk cool by standing under an inverted flowerpot in a draught in a basin of water to which half a cup of vinegar has been added.

Tunes Of Glory

One of the first commercial radio stations to open in Europe after the war was Radio Lyons. The station ran a weekly cookery programme in which tips were interspersed with music. The show was sponsored by the laxative, Bile Beans, and in 1949, a station announcer (whose embarrassment was saved by his anonymity) said cheerily over the air:

And now, thanks to Bile Beans, midnight is melody night.

Harbenger Of Cooking

A chubby, bearded little man in a striped apron named Philip Harben was the first masterchef of television. The son of two classically trained actors, he had spent much of his childhood in the kitchen and, after the war, when he served in the RAF catering division, he employed his precise and somewhat pedantic manner to excite the nation's taste buds after all the years of austerity and hardtack. Harben was an immediate success on both radio and the newly launched TV medium, instructing his listeners in a manner that brooked no argument: 'The pot to the kettle, *not* the kettle to the pot.' Although Harben always worked amid a tremendous mess because he disliked tidying, he raised the culinary expectations of millions and deservedly became the most famous cook in Britain. He was not, though, above the occasional gaffe on his live shows, and in 1949, while promoting a contest for healthy eating, he mentioned one of his favourite vegetables in a wholly unexpected context:

> *There are a number of prizes to win for the first correct answers received – all hanging like a carrot waiting to be picked.*

If Harben did not see the joke of this immediately, he had to turn away quickly from camera and busy himself with an oven, after delivering another line on a programme in August 1953 while making walnut buns:

> *Cream together well and place bun in the oven.*

Eggsasperating Moments

While Robert Harben was the undisputed first television *chef*, then the accolade of being the first television *cook* belongs to Marguerite Patten, the vivacious exponent of the culinary arts whose mixture of common sense and imagination also made her a star. Her inexpensive series of *500 Recipes . . .* books sold by the million and made her name instantly recognisable to viewers when she broke into television, offering a rather different style to her aproned rival. Marguerite's publishers were responsible for the first mistake attributed to her name in the first edition of *500 Recipes for Families* (1960):

> *Then add the milk and butter and rub the mixture well into the floor.*

Four years later she was relaxed enough to laugh at herself while demonstrating how to make a sponge cake:

> *Break the eggs carefully into a basin taking care not to break the eggs.*

Fanny By Doughlight

The other popular English television cook of this era was the autocratic Fanny Craddock whose programme mixed everyday dishes with more elaborate recipes. A woman of fierce opinions, she had been a food lover ever since she was a child: the moment in time being marked by the day when she was violently sick over her grandmother! Fanny Craddock's grandfather was, apparently, something of an eccentric, forever examining the marks on fine porcelain whenever he was at dinner parties. On one famous occasion, her grandmother turned to a horrified hostess who was watching her grandfather studying the underside of his dessert plate and said, 'Oh, don't worry, Lady Mandeville, for you know if he thought you were valuable he would turn you up and see if *you* were marked!' Always present with the star on her TV show, *Fanny Craddock*, was her monocled husband, Johnny, who invariably fawned over her. During one programme, in which she was making small pastries, he delivered perhaps the best ever cooking ad-lib:

If you're very lucky your doughnuts will come out looking like Fanny's.

French Pluck

French chef Jean Conil, whose ancestors had been cooks to the Royal Courts of France, played an important role in the introduction of his native cuisine to Britain in the fifties and sixties. He wrote on gastronomic matters for the *Daily Telegraph* and *Sunday Times*, ran his own restaurant in London and founded the International Academy of Chefs de Cuisine. Conil's knowledge of the many and varied dishes of the regions of France was also demonstrated on radio and television in programmes that were a mixture of enthusiasm and typically Gallic humour. In 1962, while promoting his latest work, *The Epicurean Book*, on BBC TV, he dropped *un gaffe* that remains a legend in television circles. He was talking about a recent visit to Normandy:

I went there, you see, to prepare a special fricken chicasee.

The Sound Of Pleasure

The American talk-show host and comedian, Steve Allen, was one of the first television stars to invite top chefs on to his top-rated NBC programme in the fifties and sixties. During conversations, Steve had a habit of substituting outlandish words for more everyday ones, and during a show in 1959 persistently used the word 'dingdong'. While talking to chef Mat Ryan he broke up the audience with the expression:

So, Mat, the way to a man's heart is through his dingdong?

Prime Air Time

General knowledge quiz shows first became popular with American viewers in the early fifties. Questions about food and cooking were a regular feature on Phil Baker's *Take It or Leave It* programme, but even this deadpan compere was unable to repress his laughter when one contestant boobed during a series of questions about comestibles, the last of which was, 'Name a noisy vegetable like celery.'

The contestant replied: 'Beans.'

The same show is also reputed to have had a young man who was asked to finish the phrase 'Peter Piper' and gabbled out:

'Pickled Peckers.'

A Famous Dish

Quiz shows such as *Take It or Leave It* did not arrive on British television screens until after the advent of the commercial stations in 1955. One of the first big successes was ITV's *Take Your Pick* hosted by the lugubrious Michael Miles. On a show in 1958 he asked one contestant: 'Russia is famous for caviar. France is famous for its *crêpes Suzette*. What is Hungary famous for?'

The man replied: 'Zsa Zsa Gabor.'

Some Like It Hot

Despite her fantastic figure, Marilyn Monroe loved food –
perhaps because her first taste of fame came as Queen of
the 1947 Artichoke Festival in Castroville, California. By
the fifties, she was hardly off the cinema or TV screens, all
the more so after her marriage in 1956 to the playwright,
Arthur Miller. Stories about her allegedly 'dumb blonde'
persona were legion: including one first related on
television. Marilyn and her husband apparently often ate
with Miller's mother who had a habit of giving them
matzo-ball soup. After about the tenth time – so the story
goes – Marilyn turned to her husband as his mother left
the room and whispered:

*Gee, Arthur, these matzo balls are pretty nice, but isn't
there any other part of the matzo you can eat?*

The Galloping Gourmet

The first cook to deliberately introduce comedy into
cooking was Graham Kerr who adopted the soubriquet
The Galloping Gourmet for himself and his daytime programme which became a world-wide success in the sixties.
Kerr's highly individual jokey patter as he demonstrated a
variety of dishes made cooking into a good giggle for many
who had never tried it before. His off-screen antics almost
matched those in front of the cameras when a series of

well-publicised affairs – to prove that cooking didn't affect the virility, he claimed – earned him many headlines. Two of Graham Kerr's ad-libs also made news. The first was in 1964 when he announced:

> *I've decided to play my next recipe by ear – when you're married, it's about the only thing left to play with.*

Eighteen months later, on a programme devoted to fish dishes, he was talking about squid and observed with a grin:

> *A squid, as you know of course, has ten testicles.*

Spaghetti A La Fred

Graham Kerr may well have run the first comedy cooking series, but Spike Milligan had already written kitchen sketches for his famous radio series, *The Goons*, and subsequently for *A Show Called Fred* (1956) – a programme that would ultimately inspire *Monty Python* and *Fawlty Towers*. In every show a custard pie was ritually applied to the pretty face of singer, Patti Lewis, and culinary jokes flew thick and fast. In one of the funniest episodes in the third series, *The Best of Fred*, Milligan cooked his 'Spaghetti a la Fred':

> *Take a strand of spaghetti, lay it face downwards on a marble slab. Run a compass over the strand and find its magnetic North. Roll the strand in a solution of beaten egg yolk and Volnay '47. Take finely sliced garlic and pack*

carefully on each side of the spaghetti strand. Take a copper pan, fill with water, boil to 180°F or 201°C. Add a handful of salt. Drop strand into boiling water for 15 minutes. When cooked to 'al dente' remove strand and serve with 3 fried eggs — mushrooms in wine sauce — chipolatas, steak, etc., etc.

Musical Dreams

One of the most popular guests on the Arthur Godfrey TV programme in the sixties was the singer and actor, Walter Slezak, famous for his Tony-award-winning performance in the Broadway show, *Fanny*, and a noted gourmet who often passed on recipes to viewers. In November 1964, he was introduced to a fellow guest, Faye Emerson, who broke up the audience with her opening remark:

Walter Slezak! Whenever I think of you, I think of your Fanny.

Fork Standards

Described as 'The Woman Who changed the Face of Middle Class Kitchens' and 'Keeper of the National Palate', Elizabeth David was the cookery writer who brought sunshine, aubergines and olive oil into British kitchens through her articles and books on Mediterranean cooking. A rebel from childhood, she was first an actress before living an exotic life in Europe where she had several love affairs and began writing the idiosyncratic recipes that made her reputation: 'The cockscombs must be cooked for an hour in salted water and skinned.' Interviewed by Derek Cooper on *The Food Programme* and asked how it felt to be the greatest food writer of the century, she replied, after a long pause, 'I don't know – you tell me.' Elizabeth David disliked personal publicity, but her recipes were frequently used on the television and radio, like this example from 1967. Though mangled by the presenter, it still has the aroma of her inimitable style:

The principal thing to remember when preparing a fork supper is to select only food which can be eaten comfortably on a plate with a fork. In the winter, hot bouillon or clear soup is always popular and can well be included.

Lines To Die For

In the early years of television in America when many programmes were transmitted live, the sponsors of the shows often had their advertising messages read out by the star of the show or an announcer. Not surprisingly – and despite the best efforts of the professionals – errors in pronunciation and fluffed lines were not uncommon. Here are a dozen classic examples of mangled moments – or bloopers as they became known – all with a culinary flavour. No wonder they left the presenters covered with confusion:

CAMPBELL'S SOUPS (Announcer: Del Sharbet, 1972) *'So, ladies, be sure and go to your corner grocer*

and stock up with Campbell's Green Split Poo Seep.'
CHIFFON MARGARINE (Announcer: Barney Dean, 1966) *'If you think it's butter, well it's snot, it's Chiffon.'*
CHOCK FULL OF NUTS (Announcer: Morey Amsterdam) *'You will enjoy a Jock Full of Nuts Special at lunchtime.'*
FLORIDA LEMON JUICE (Announcer: Jay Stevens, 1970) *'This delicious lemon juice is not concentrated or reconstituted – it's just squeezed from fresh, juicy oranges.'*
GRAHAMS' CRACKERS (Announcer: Paul Stanley, 1969) *'So don't forget to stock up on Grahams' Crappers.'*
HOVIS BREAD (Announcer: Ed Murdoch, 1966) *'Do you know how the sandwich got its name? The Earl of Sandwich was the first man to put his meat between two pieces of bread.'*
KELLOGG'S CORNFLAKES (Announcer: Dick Clark, 1967) *'Try this delicious breast food every morning.'*
KENTUCKY FRIED CHICKEN (Announcer: Bill Witherdale, 1970) *'So, folks, if you are looking for the easy way to enjoy your dinner this Sunday, just drop by the Colonel's place for delicious, finger lickin' Kenfucky fried chicken.'*
KRAFT CHEESE (Announcer: Howard Smith, 1973) *'Ladies, remember to add this delicious cheese to your shopping list – it's Kraft's Roquefart Cheese.'*
PLANTER'S PEANUTS (Announcer: Joan Schaffer) *'Remember, folks, be sure to ask for Southern-planted roasted penis.'*
SEALTEST ICE CREAM (Announcer: Mort Zamarino, 1968) *'Delicious, fresh, tasty ice cream for*

you and your family – always ask for Sealtest horny strawberry.'

WONDER BREAD (Announcer: Arthur Mulligan, 1961) *'Dad will love the delicious flavour, too. So, remember, it's Wonder Bread for the breast in bed.'*

A Loose Moment

The legendary host of the American *Tonight Show*, Johnny Carson, which ran from 1962 and attracted the biggest names in show business and politics, was not above the odd mistake. In the early days, Johnny delivered some of the commercials himself, including these two classics in 1964. The first was for Jolly Green Giant vegetables:

Have you ever walked out of your house and found yourself face to face with a huge green fruit?

And the second was for a certain well-known cathartic:

Here's how to relieve an upsex stomach. I mean an upsep stomach. With Sex-law . . . Ex-lax!

Potty Madness

Merv Griffin, Johnny Carson's great rival in the US as a talk-show host, was responsible for another classic blooper. One of his guests on *The Merve Griffin Show* in

1965 was telling him just what a poor cook his wife was and what he planned to do, when – enter foot into mouth:

I've bought her a new crackpot to cook in.

Henny And The Chicks

Henny Youngman was another of the leading US television stars who had his own comedy series as well as appearing on a variety of other programmes. He was a master of the one-line joke, and was himself once comically announced as 'The Laugh King of the One-Winer'. The newspapers had a field day with him and his name after this peak-hour gaffe in a commercial transmitted in 1965:

Houchens Market has fresh young hens ready for the rooster . . . I mean roaster.

Juice Power

Mike Douglas – no relative of the famous film star, Michael Douglas – was for years the host of a popular daytime talk programme, *The Mike Douglas Show*, syndicated across America. In 1967 he had as a guest the very fey, falsetto-voiced pop singer, Tiny Tim, who told the viewing audience that he had just lost forty pounds on a diet of onions and prune juice. Without missing a beat, Douglas commented:

Well, that ought to keep you moving.

The Smell Test

Julia Child was one of the first American cookery experts to become a nationwide favourite when she presented a series, *The French Chef*, during the fifties and sixties, not to mention writing several ground-breaking books on gourmet food. A lively, enthusiastic lady, she sometimes let her tongue run away with her as in these two instances from the late sixties:

   * *It's best to go to the fish market early Friday morning and leave your odor . . .*
   * *Then you add two forkfuls of cooking oil . . .*

Frozen Out

Housewife's Choice was a rather proper daily TV programme in the US which ran in the sixties. The show featured hints on cooking and on one unhappy day in 1964, presenter Jennifer Leake got into all sorts of trouble while discussing the best ways of preparing meat for freezing. She ended with some advice on storing joints and how to cook them later. Miss Leake said, smiling:

So, ladies, when you need it, go take your meat out of the freezer and beat it.

A Hot Point To Watch

The CBS game show, *The Price is Right*, hosted by Bill Cullen, in which contestants had to guess the value of items of merchandise, was a great success in America from the late fifties. In 1984 it came to Britain, hosted by Leslie Crowther, whose expression, 'Come on down', became a universal catch phrase. Cookery items were a regular feature in both the British and American versions, but it was Bill Cullen who stumbled into this goof in 1973 when reading out the list of prizes to a young housewife:

And to help you with your cooking, we are giving away an assortment of electric saucepans, frying pans and a Dutch oven with a girdle.

Pulling The Other One

Both British and American TV viewers have enjoyed deliberately cooked-up culinary capers. Over the years, *Candid Camera*, the notorious peepshow which originated in the US in the fifties with its aptly-named presenter Alan Funt (it was later introduced into Britain in the mischievous hands of Jonathan Routh) set people up in kitchens, restaurants, bars and, on one notable occasion, in an Automat Diner in New York. After inserting their money and removing a dish of food from a sealed compartment, dumbstruck victims saw an item of food whipped off their plates by a piece of string and back behind the glass. Some patiently repeated the exercise unaware they were being filmed. Undoubtedly, though, the classic gastronomic giggle was perpetrated on April Fools' Day in 1957 by Richard Dimbleby, the presenter of the BBC's prestigious documentary programme, *Panorama*. Amid stories of political upheaval and national crisis from all over the world, he introduced an item about an unexpectedly heavy crop of spaghetti growing at Ticino on the borders of Switzerland and Italy which had resulted from 'one of the mildest winters in living memory and the virtual disappearance of the spaghetti weevil', Dimbleby explained. He was filmed strolling between trees groaning with the crop and watching pickers taking down strands and laying them out to dry in the sun. He concluded, 'For those who love this dish, there's nothing like home-grown spaghetti!' The gravitas with which Richard Dimbleby delivered his lines left millions of viewers convinced the story was true – until the realisation of what day it was set in. The next morning, following numerous phone calls, the BBC issued a statement which admitted cooking up the hoax, but still managed to squeeze out one last joke:

The BBC has also received requests from people wishing to know how they can grow their own spaghetti. The advice of our experts is to place a sprig of spaghetti in a tin of tomato sauce and hope for the best.

Funday Flavours

There have been lots of other April Fool jokes with a culinary flavour. In 1982, for example, BBC Radio Wales told listeners that there were plans afoot to produce bacon-flavoured cheese from sows' milk; while in 1985, the *British Philatelic Bulletin* claimed that a new issue of stamps would have flavoured gum: the English would taste of roast beef, the Welsh of leek, the Irish of bacon and the Scottish of porridge. Housewives in Spalding, Lincolnshire, were asked to leave used tea bags outside their homes in 1987 to be collected and recycled through a 'reflavourising machine' – dozens did – and a large number of women in the Suffolk village of Bildeston who turned up to claim 'Free Butter' in 2000 also found the joke had gone sour. Perhaps, though, the most amusing of all came from Zimbabwe, reported in *The Herald* in 1983, which informed readers:

A potential world-record athlete has been found who trains by racing railway engines and eats rhinoceros fat and baobab root, but can only run clockwise around the track.

Off Their Crockers

Although there is nothing funny about the Betty Crocker flour mixes which are so popular with American housewives, the good lady herself is actually a figment of the imagination. When the manufacturers, Gold Medal, first launched their flour, a national picture puzzle competition was run to promote it and attracted over 30,000 responses. Many of these required a personal reply – but the question was, who should sign them? After a brain-storming session by the Gold Medal staff, the surname of a recently retired director was chosen along with the cosy-sounding Christian name of a secretary. Since then, 'Betty Crocker' has been seen on all the company's products as well as innumerable cookery books and recipe cards – making her the most famous cook in America who never was. Recipes prepared in the special kitchens maintained by the company to test new products have often been used on shows sponsored by the company. In one in 1966, the following announcement was made:

Good morning, ladies, our baking recipe today features another delicious Betty Crocker cake mix special. We are sure your entire family will enjoy this Betty Baker crock mix delight.

Slip Of The Tongue

The publication in 1964 of *Great Dishes of the World* by Robert Carrier marked the arrival of the modern, full-colour cookbook. Selling over two million copies in 12 languages, it earned its author the accolade of being the great showman of British cooking. Carrier subsequently introduced cookery cards, opened his own cookshops and restaurants, and became the star of his own cookery series as well as a guest on many other TV shows. Even as his fame continued to grow, Carrier was still the victim of the occasional journalistic clanger, as in the William Hickey column of the *Daily Express* in October 1967:

He has a weakness for English food, especially paté de foie gras.

Pear Belle Zena

The vivacious cook Zena Skinner had a popular cookery programme on BBC Television in the late sixties. A great fan of natural foods, she regularly featured recipes for fruits when they were in season. In September 1967, Zena prepared several dishes made from pears, during the course of which she instructed her viewers:

Take some eating pears, peel them, and cook them slowly standing in water flavoured with a vanilla pod.

73

The Cartland *Mélange*

Barbara Cartland, the vision in pink, described as 'The World's Favourite Romantic Novelist', was a frequent guest on television chat shows. Healthy eating was a subject on which she could be relied upon to hold forth and she was also never slow with advice on how to spice up viewers' love lives. In 1972 Barbara appeared in an interview on ITV and delivered the following strenuous guide to better bonking:

An enormous number of people stop being sexy early in life because they are not eating the right things. White sugar is the curse of civilisation – it causes fatigue and sexual apathy between husband and wife. My recipe against sexual fatigue is to take honey in large quantities, 2 Gev-E tablets, 10 vitamin E pills, 4 wheat-germ oil tablets, 4 vitamin A pills, 4 bone-meal tablets, 6 liver-plus tablets, 2 dessert spoonfuls of Bio Strath Elixir, twice a day.

Cereal Killer

Live television advertising has rarely been seen since the seventies, though making commercials can still be beset with problems – especially where food is concerned. Gaffs have been blown time and again while actors and actresses have been shooting films for any number of products. The record number of takes for a food commercial is believed to be held by the actress Pat Coombs who forgot the name of one item 28 times during filming. Interviewed in 1973 some months after the disaster had become common knowledge, Pat told a *Daily Mirror* reporter:

I just couldn't remember anything beyond the fact it was a kind of Swiss breakfast cereal. Shortly afterwards it was withdrawn. I no longer eat, er . . . ['muesli', the reporter prompted].

Chinese Favourite

Victor Sassie was for years one of the most famous restaurateurs in London, noted for his perfectionism and endlessly sought for his advice by the makers of cookery programmes on radio and television. He was also a man of great good humour who, while being interviewed on *Late Night Lineup* in 1978, told a classic *faux pas* story against himself. It concerned a dinner party he had run for a well-known peer in honour of the Chinese Ambassador. The party included six distinguished Britons and four Chinese diplomats, for whom Sassie produced a four-course meal. At the end of the dinner, the Ambassador thanked the restaurateur – through an interpreter – for having included several of his favourite ingredients, especially wild cherry soup and white capsicums. At this, Sassie whispered to the interpreter:

Please tell His Excellency, I am most grateful and happy to have found a chink in the armour.

Space Rations

With the coming of the space age, there has been increasing discussion about the diet of astronauts. Initially, no one was sure whether a peckish space traveller would be able to swallow in zero gravity, and as early as 1939 the British Interplanetary Society was recommending that astronauts should be, 'Fattened up in advance and while in flight given a daily pound of butter to fulfil their calorific needs.' In the sixties, astronauts like John Glenn labelled the freeze-dried and vacuum-packed high-protein food he was given as 'mush in a tube' and demanded a sandwich as soon as he landed. The main problem has been identified as making food palatable and not tasting like 'rancid almonds' as the French astronaut Jean-Loup Chretien described the Russian pre-packed pot noodles he ate on the Mir space station. (It was later revealed that the grub was so bad the Russian cosmonauts came close to mutiny.) Another Frenchman, Richard Filippi, was so appalled that he has devised a culinary art called 'gastronautics' to try to ensure that future space travellers will eat well. On television, however, scenes of men in space eating have usually inspired admiration rather than amusement – although this was not the case in July 1975 when the American Apollo and Russian Soyuz spacecrafts docked and viewers were able to see the crews working and sharing time together. An excited BBC news presenter, Frank McGee, told viewers to the *Nine O'Clock News*:

I have just learned that we do have film of the astronauts' breakfast, which will be coming up shortly.

Service With A Figurine

Welsh sculptress Beryl Cheame became well known in the seventies for her various art forms based on food. But she completely amazed her fellow members of the Welsh Arts Council Sculpture Committee at a luncheon in 1975 with a set of crockery moulded from parts of her body. She later told *Wales Today*:

> *I got the idea during a dinner party. All at once I realised what a marvellous food container the body is. I used my breasts to mould the soup dishes and my stomach for the plates. Later I added a casserole which was formed around a cast of my behind.*

A Thickening Mixture

The British comedian, Larry Grayson, with his catch-phrase, 'Shut that door!' was the first person to deliberately suggest a gay persona on television. He also attracted millions of fans to the *Larry Grayson Show* with endless stories about his friend, Everard, including one monologue in 1976 in which the pair set about cooking a meal – a task at which the comedian was reputed to be skilled. It was the camp Grayson who handed out the advice to his friend:

> *Beat the egg yolk and add the milk. Then slowly blend in*

the sifted flour. As you do, you can see the mixture is sickening. Oh, silly me! I meant thickening. Thorry.

All Steamed Up

Viewers of ITV news in October 1978 were startled to see picket lines outside one of London's leading hotels, Claridge's. According to the commentary, this state of affairs had come about because of a storm over casseroles. A trainee chef named Richard Elvidge had been dismissed by the management, but his colleagues had walked out on strike in sympathy. The dispute was resolved without the spilling of too much salt, however, and Elvidge went off to run his own restaurant in Scunthorpe. His moment of fame also earned him a cookery column in the *Scunthorpe Star* in which he wrote about a number of regional favourites, including suet pudding:

> *There are some people who cannot make a suet pudding successfully. These are better steamed.*

Holy Orders

The ebullient Reverend John Eley of Cambridge brought a new dimension to the culinary arts with his series of TV programmes, *The Cooking Canon* and *The Cooking Canon Entertains* in the eighties. The jolly, bearded churchman with his apron and dog collar prepared a variety of dishes ranging from brawn to pigeon pie and gave suggestions for elegant dinner parties. The Reverend also loved his vegetables, but a reprint of one of his televised menus in *The Scotsman* in August 1985 suffered from a painful misprint:

Instead of mint on buttered new toes, try some chopped dill leaves. Use them also for garnishing chilled tomato soup, as a change from basil.

Gastronomic Gaffes

It's not only the chefs and cookery experts who get their words wrong or their metaphors mixed when they are broadcasting. Here are half a dozen examples from some very well-known names overheard on the radio:

She has finally tasted the sweet smell of success. DAVID COLEMAN, BBC 2.
It was a whole new can of beans in every sense of the word. SIMON BATES, Radio 1.
That's a fish of a different feather. DEREK JAMESON, Radio 2.
I wish I'd had the hot-dog concession – they'd have sold like hot cakes. WALLY WHYTON, Radio 2.
He went down like a sack of potatoes, then made a meal of it. TREVOR BROOKING, Radio 2.
That's the gravy on the cake. BARBARA POTTER, Radio 2.

Spinning A Tail

Broadcaster and novelist Judy Bosh made headline news in 1982 with what she called 'one of my wilder inspirations' – trout cooked in dishwater. The story began in the pages of *Home & Freezer Digest* in February 1982, where she described her new way with fish:

> *I get large trout from a fish farm and tuck them into the place for cups on the top rack – square fish are better than long fish. I set the dish-washer to the normal plate-washing programme and in fifty minutes the trout are perfectly cooked.*

Yorkshire Relish

The long-running BBC TV series, *Last of the Summer Wine*, featuring the comic adventures of three elderly, retired friends in a Yorkshire village, who spend much of their time in a small café, inspired one of the entrants in a competition for hospital chefs in the south of England in 1982. The *Oxford Mail* ran details of the event in its issue of 11 October:

> *The contest included the following entries: the characters of Compo, Foggy and Clegg from* Last of the Summer Wine *'brought to life in margarine'; a chicken in the form of a chess board 'surrounded by chess men mounted on*

eggs'; and a Jersey pullet disguised as a frog about to leap off the plate. A spokesman said, 'It is the job of a hospital chef to tempt people to eat.'

Eggsactly Right

Food With The Famous is just one of the highly acclaimed books Jane Grigson has written about food and cooking. Brought up in the North East of England with its tradition for good eating, she began to tickle the taste buds of readers writing in the *Observer Colour Magazine* in the late sixties, and her highly individual recipes have been frequently discussed on radio and television programmes. In 1985, she amused her many admirers with this observation:

Buy really good eggs, preferably from hens that you know, one per person.

The Ageing Process

Jane Grigson's daughter, Sophie, has also proved herself a chip off the old block with her cookery column in the London *Evening Standard*, several books and television series for Channel 4. Giving advice in a column about the preparation of Christmas puddings in October 1988, she wrote:

Today the Christmas pudding can be cooked in a micro-wave oven in just minutes and retain all the flavour, texture and appearance of grandmothers.

The Gravy Strain

The Danish pianist and comedian, Victor Borge, who starred in his own one-man TV show throughout the seventies, loved talking about food. On one programme he paused from playing the piano and told the audience that an uncle of his had once tried to make a fortune by crossing a sponge with an Idaho potato. He continued:

It tasted awful, but it sure held a lot of gravy.

Finger Dipping

Marco Pierre White, the Yorkshire-born chef who came to national attention in the late eighties for his fiery behaviour with staff and customers alike, is also acknowledged as one of the finest cooks of his time. A towering figure well over six feet tall with a great mane of hair, his passionate love of food and almost manic search for perfection has made him a natural for television in *Take Six Cooks* and his own series, *Marco*. A renowned practical joker – he once organised four of his chefs to tip buckets of pig slop, flour and water over an intrusive gossip columnist and photographer – he also likes to talk about the aphrodisiac properties of good cooking and told *Taste* magazine in June 1982:

If people want to eat with their fingers, I'm not going to tell them to stop. I think table-cloths are like sheets – the more mess, the more those people have enjoyed it.

Surprise Packets

The rumpled figure of Keith Floyd, cooking utensil in one hand and glass of wine in the other, dominated the nineties with his 16 television series and 18 books, varying in subjects from *Floyd on Fish* to *Floyd on Hangovers*. A chance meeting with BBC producer David Pritchard – who Floyd refers to as 'a big man with a voracious appetite for food and pints of Bass' (a description that almost fits himself) – led to the launching of the TV series which took the pair all over the world and made Floyd a household name as he rustled up meals in the unlikeliest places. His rumbustious manner and headline-making exploits have made him something of a cult figure who can be relied upon to be full of surprises when on television. On one occasion, when describing a forthcoming series, he joked, 'The booze will be flowing like wine.' In *Far Flung Floyd* (1990) he explained that, because his birthday was close to Christmas, his mother used to send him packets of home-made faggots and peas – the number of packets increasing each year with his age:

In America when I talked about this to Eartha Kitt on her show, she burst out laughing and asked how on earth I could get away with saying to viewers, 'I had 48 faggots this Christmas.'

Catching Haggis

The success of the BBC programme, *Masterchef*, launched in 1990, was such that it soon became known as 'the Olympic Games of home cooking' and made a star of its presenter, Loyd Grossman. The series, in which ordinary men and women competed for the honour of being named the best amateur chef, also became a show-case for Grossman with his strangulated mid-Atlantic vowels and long-drawn-out sounds as he drooled over food. Among the most memorable dishes to feature on the programme was haggis, about which Grossman commented in April 1992:

I have been told it can be served with Orkney clapshot which is a mixture of swede and potato – but that rather sounds like something you catch.

Among the guests on *Masterchef* was the equally lugubrious Derek Nimmo who talked about his favourite dish in July 1991:

My favourite way of eating oysters, which I do in Muscat, is to swim into the Indian Ocean with half a bottle of Möet et Chandon strapped to my leg. I swim out to the rocks, prise the oysters from the rocks, eat them live, squealing as they go down, and then drink the champagne.

Stiffening The Resolve

Another lover of oysters is the TV personality and *Punch* columnist on food, Clement Freud. He has written about the tasty molluscs on several occasions, and in one memorable article in 1995 made special mention of the aphrodisiac qualities to be found in a plate of a dozen:

I recommend that you swallow them quickly. If you don't do so your neck will go stiff.

Delia's Delicacies

Described as 'The Mrs Beeton of our times', Delia Smith is Britain's best-selling cookery author and her television programmes attract millions of viewers every year. A quietly spoken, vivacious lady, her other passion apart from cooking is football and her culinary success has enabled her to become the major shareholder in her local team, Norwich City. Despite the preciseness of her instructions in her programmes, Delia has dropped the odd clanger, telling viewers in 1998:

To prevent tears when peeling onions, either bite on a slice of bread or work under a running tap and breathe through the mouth.

In the press, she fell victim to the printer's devil as early as June 1980 in this entry in the *Daily Express'* TV listings which managed to muddle her with the Charles Bronson movie, *11 Harrowhouse*:

3.55. Delia Smith's Cookery Course.
One of the most ingenious robberies of all time is planned.

Her own local paper, the *East Anglian Daily Times*, even made a fudge of one of her big days in May, 2000:

Delia Smith's brassiere was opened at Norwich City football ground on Saturday. Delia, 58, said she was relieved and delighted by the reaction.

And, finally, there was the story of a hopeless cook who was given six copies of Delia's latest book by different friends that Christmas. A report in the *Yorkshire Post* of 31 December 2000 stated:

Louise Preston, 32, from Skipton, North Yorkshire, cooks salad in the microwave and once made her husband some ham sandwiches – but forgot to put in the ham. Friends decided to send her the Delia Smith after she resolved to improve. Her husband Alex said, 'A cook book is the last thing you'd think of getting Louise. She struggled with my packed lunch.'

Too Many Cooks

Ready, Steady, Cook, another long-running cookery show in which professional chefs and invited viewers cook meals

against the clock, has also produced its fair share of gastronomic giggles. The show was devised by Peter Bazalgette
after reading a report that most people cooked their
evening meal in 20 minutes for less than £5. Originally
launched in 1994, the show was initially presented by Fern
Britton, but more recently by Ainsley Harriott, a former
stand-up comedian. *Ready, Steady, Cook* has made stars of
its chefs and together they've also proved too many cooks
can spoil the broth – or at least make a joke out of it as
these examples demonstrate:

FERN BRITTON (To Brian Turner): *I would pick on
a chef who can lick me.*
AINSLEY 'What's he like?' HARRIOTT (To
diminutive guest, the former ballet dancer, Wayne
Sleep): *Now get your nuts on the tray.* To which Sleep
replied, *Not with my size, I can't.*
ANTHONY 'The Arsonist' WORRELL (To
viewers): *My philosophy is a bit of dirt never did anyone
any harm.*
BRIAN 'I Hate Puds' TURNER (A bleeped
moment): *Not a lemon turd tart at any price!*
PATRICK 'Inspector Gadget' ANTHONY (Another
bleeped moment): *Did he call my show* Patrick's Pantie?

One Rhode Too Many

The spiky-haired Gary Rhodes is another of the new
generation of celebrity English chefs with his own TV
show and a string of best-selling books to his name. He
travels a great deal for his work and in October 2000 was

asked by Sarah Tucker of *The Times* what was the weirdest thing he had ever eaten:

> *I was a guest on a US morning TV show and the chef cooked me something with crocodile. It was so tough. I couldn't speak – and I couldn't swallow it.*

Meals On Wheels

Probably the most surprising television success of the nineties was *Two Fat Ladies* in which two large, upper-class ladies, Jennifer Paterson and Clarissa Dickson-Wright, careered about the English countryside in a motorcycle and side-car chatting about cooking and demonstrating recipes. It was an unlikely enough hit in Britain, but caught on in America and Australia, too. Jennifer had begun working as cook, odd-job woman and office mascot at the *Spectator* and catered for a whole range of luncheon guests from Enoch Powell to Barry Humphreys (who left the room towards the end of one meal and reappeared as Dame Edna Everage), as well as writing a weekly column which mirrored the magazine's sense of fun and zest for the good life. Her irreverent charm and louche, politically incorrect style made her a favourite with readers and television audiences alike. Her cry of 'I'll shout at whomever I like!' was legendary as was her utterance at a riotous party raided by the police: 'Here are the fuzz! Have some fizz!' Funnier still is this so-typical observation of one particular meal made to camera on *Two Fat Ladies*:

I had a dear little maize-fed poussin stuffed with lobster and ginger served with a choron sauce – very good indeed. The most lovely scent of tarragon and ginger assailed the nostrils when unplugging the first piece of lobster from the bird's cavity.

Clarissa Dickson-Wright, the other half of the team, was the perfect foil with a matching sense of humour and passion for cookery. Wherever the two went there were always gales of laughter and mountains of good food. Clarissa also delivered a classic tale of humour to the series:

We all know 'an army marches on its stomach', but what about Attila the Hun's men, who found a novel way of curing meat as they rode to battle? They put pieces of fresh meat under their saddles and, as they rode, the salt from the horse's sweat and the bouncing of the rider combined to dry and cure the meat!

Five Bellies Pie

Probably the most revolting recipe ever described on television was given by the footballer Paul Gascoigne when he appeared on Channel 4's *TFI Friday* hosted by Chris Evans in January 1998. Gazza was accompanied by his 22-stone friend, Jimmy 'Five Bellies' Gardner, and recounted the story of a holiday the pair had recently spent in Italy. They had returned to the villa where they were staying after a very liquid evening and the Geordie prankster decided to doctor a meat pie before serving it to his friend. Gascoigne explained to Evans:

There was a couple of stray cats at the villa and I took the mince out of this pie, got hold of the cats' poo, and mixed it together. I put it in the microwave. The smell was unbelievable, but because he was drunk he didn't know. He even told me, 'That's one of the best pies I've ever had.'

On Top Down Under

The man in charge of catering at the Olympic Games in Sydney in August 2000 was Antony Sweetapple, as much in demand by the media as by the appetites of the athletes he was trying to feed. Operating a 4,900-seater main dining hall for over 10,000 competitors, each able to pick from 1,700 main dishes from all over the world, Sweetapple was asked just how big a challenge this represented by a reporter from the TV programme *Sydney Today* on 26 August. Sweetapple was lucky to stumble over only one word:

We're probably the biggest restaurant in the world. On average we're producing 48,000 meals a day and at peak times about 60,000. We fired our first shit in anger last month with 2,500 people going through in 45 minutes.

Grabbing The Aubergine

Gordon Ramsey, who was named Chef of the Year 2000 by the catering industry, is a man with a blazing temper and even fiercer politically incorrect opinions about cooking. A former professional footballer turned chef, Gordon became familiar to the world at large in a TV documentary, *Boiling Point*, in which his volatile nature – described by some jealous rivals as 'the Gordon Ramsey school of charm' – was exposed as, too, were his brilliant culinary skills. Having worked with Marco Pierre White, Gordon knows all about a demanding chef and has aired his views in the press and on several TV programmes. In September 2000 he got into hot water for a remark about female chefs:

Suppose you're going out with some girl who's 25, pretty, and she's spent the day sticking her fingers up the arse of a pigeon to bring out its guts. I mean, if I said, 'How's your day been?' and she said, 'Chef got me doing two boxes of pigeons, I had to blow-torch the wings off, then I had to stick my fingers up their arse, pull their hearts out, chop them up and finish them as a sauce' and then those hands have got to grip my aubergine five hours later, I don't think that would do much for my sex life.

Pukka Nosh

Jamie Oliver, the hyperactive young Essex-born chef, is regarded by some critics as the unlikely heir to Delia Smith as the most popular cook on television. Even his 'high-octane yoof' attitude to gastronomic matters cannot disguise his talent as he demonstrated on his series, *The Naked Chef* – a reference to the way his cooking is stripped back to simple ingredients rather than his appearance. A publican's son and former assistant chef at the River Cafe,

Jamie's madcap antics in the kitchen and his high-speed estuary English using words like 'geezer', 'malarky', 'wicked' and 'pukka' have endeared him to viewers of all ages. In fact, he always has a flash of wit or two for the cameras or the press, as he showed just before his marriage in June 2000: 'On the morning of the wedding we are going to get up early and bake loads of different breads – it's quite an emotional thing for me because it feels like the last bread I'll make before I start thinking about putting a real bun in the oven.' Jamie has been just as amusing on *The Naked Chef*, declaring in August 2000:

> *I'd eat human flesh easily. Slice it very thinly, add some shallots, a bit of lemon, capers, Parmesan – top!*

A week after this he was in the Peterborough gossip column in the *Daily Telegraph*:

> *Jamie Oliver's fame hasn't reached the yeomen of South Torfrey. A local butcher recently told farmers in the Devon village that a 'nude chef' was to descend on them in search of chickens. Police were promptly put on their guard against the poultry-stealing flasher – but Oliver was innocently stocking up his new Knightsbridge restaurant, Monte's!*

4

Feud For Thought

The manic attempts by Basil Fawlty to hide a suspect kipper down the front of his pullover and avoid any mention of the war in front of some German guests in his restaurant, were just two classic moments in the television comedy, *Fawlty Towers*, the saga of the worst-run hotel in Britain. Although the series featuring the apoplectic owner and his hapless staff only lasted a few years in the late seventies, it was recently voted the best British TV show of all time – and is still being re-run all over the world. John Cleese, who created the crackpot establishment – which rudely anagrammed its name weekly from *Fawlty Towers* to *Fatty Owls* and *Farty Towels* – made no secret that the script was based on real-life experience which occurred in the late sixties, while filming *Monty Python's Flying Circus*, when he and his co-stars stayed at the Gleneagles Hotel in Torquay. According to Cleese, the proprietor subsequently emigrated.

The truth is, though, that places like *Fawlty Towers* are to be found all over the world. Establishments where the proprietor seems as prone to mishaps as Basil; the waiters as incompetent as Manuel, that 'waste of space from Barcelona'; and the food about as fresh as the dead guest hidden in the hotel's laundry basket. Such stories as *can* be printed about these Faulty Towers will be found in this chapter. And, appropriately, to start with here is a small add from a Devonshire newspaper which appeared in 1975:

DETACHED PRIVATE HOTEL. Excellently situated near Torquay Sea Front. Practically on the level.

Out Of The Frying Pan

The celebrated scene where Basil Fawlty thrashed his recalcitrant Austin 1100 with a branch as he tried to extricate himself from yet another catering calamity was recalled in June 1985 when the police in Cologne came to the aid of a driver of an equally ageing saloon car. The officers found that the vehicle belonging to a local restaurateur, Ernst Banik, was not what it seemed, according to a report in *Die Welt*:

> *Herr Banik has cut the cost of motoring by running the car on old potato chip fat. He clocks up 17,000 miles a year on 1,100 gallons of vegetable oil drained from his chip fryer. The fuel gives off a smell of stale chips.*

A Stiff Brew

The owner of a 1962 Austin Princess hearse was brought before Harrogate Court in January 1975. According to a report in the *Yorkshire Evening Post*, Albert Simpson was charged with causing an obstruction on the public highway, but explained to the magistrates:

> *I am a bit of an inventor. I bought the hearse with the idea of converting it into a mobile tea shop – but I am afraid the venture has led me into trouble.*

Chinese Cracker

A small Chinese restaurant in Penrith became famous with locals and tourists alike because of the eccentricity of one of its waiters during the heyday of *Fawlty Towers*. The man's expressions were often compared to those of the hapless Manuel – and one found its way into the pages of the *Sunday Post*, courtesy of a letter from Nora Lindsay of Greenock:

> *It was the appetizing smell of chips that drew us to the restaurant. We hadn't much time, so I asked the immaculate waiter if we could carry out. He looked puzzled. I tried again, speaking slowly. Did they have carry-outs? 'Ah,' he said, brightening. 'We have curry chicken. Curry rice. But we have no curry oot.'*

Batter Padding

Another Chinese restaurant in Norwich, Norfolk, was also the subject of a mixture of amazement and amusement when its owner was brought before magistrates in March 1986. The *Eastern Daily Press* recorded the man's offence in a single paragraph:

> *Mr Yan Sang Chan, the owner of the Dragon Super-kitchen in Norwich, has been fined for stirring a vat of curry with a cricket bat.*

Accent On Food

Police in Wakefield, West Yorkshire, were told in September 2000 about the disappearance from a Chinese restaurant of a budgerigar that recited the menu in a Chinese accent. The *Daily Telegraph* carried a report of the loss of the female bird, known as China, which could also ask whether customers wanted rice or chips:

She escaped from her cage and has since been spotted several times. An angler tried to coax her out of a tree to be met with the reply: 'What you want? Prawn cracker?'

Fighting Fire With Curry

A Chinese restaurant in the picturesque little town of Crewkerne, Somerset, was said to have resembled a scene from *Fawlty Towers* on an evening in November 1976, when customers and waiters began to fight after an argument broke out over the order in which tables were being served. A report in the *Western Gazette* describe the scene:

During a running battle at the restaurant in Crewkerne, flowerpots were hurled towards members of the staff who returned the fire with ladles of hot curry.

Flying Tonight

The sight of long queues forming outside the Singing Sun restaurant in Beijing even before it was open caught the attention of the Chinese authorities in 1996 – especially because the restaurant had a reputation for bad food. Health officials joined the throng and one duly reported, 'The donkey is tough, the sauces greasy and the rest of the food tastes like dog's dirt, yet customers still go back day after day.' When the proprietor Chen Tai-si was brought before the district court, the reason for the establishment's extraordinary attraction was revealed, a report in the *Weekly World News* stated. Chen Tai-si confessed:

After someone threw their dinner through the window, I decided to begin adding my special seasoning to every dish. They do such things as a matter of course in the West and I got the idea from a chef called Mrs Beeton. I was doing my countrymen a service. Just because I put pure opium paste in my dishes does not mean I am a criminal.

Adding A Bit Of Bite

A curry-eating contest in Llandrindod Wells in December 1994 gave a whole new meaning to the expression of there being bite in a good curry. The fracas which occurred in the restaurant was reported by the *Radnor County Times & Gazette* when Bernard Davies was brought before the town's magistrates court to answer a charge of assault causing actual bodily harm. According to the report, Davies had removed his false teeth while competing against Martin Harding and placed them on the table:

The dentures became an object of mirth, it was stated, one man putting them in his own mouth while another dropped his trousers. The prosecution alleged that Davies had put the false teeth between the trouserless man's buttocks. This was denied by Timothy Van Rees (defending) who maintained it had been done by Mr Harding. The false teeth, however, had become lost, the curry-eating contest was abandoned, and Davies was alleged to have attacked his opponent. Speaking in mitigation Mr Van Rees said: 'When you suffer the indignity of having your false teeth jammed between the cheeks of someone else's bottom, it makes the most mild-mannered person lose his temper.'

False Pretences

A disturbance in a Dutch restaurant, The Spui, in The Hague in April 1989 was also generated by false teeth and led to an appearance in court. Explaining how the events had begun, the proprietor, Carl Winteers, said that a customer had come in for a sandwich but was unable to eat it because his new dentures were hurting. At this, another customer, Mr Wim Pieters, had taken out his own false teeth and offered them to the newcomer. A report in the *Haagsche Courant* reported Winteers's subsequent statement to the police:

The teeth were not a perfect fit, but were much better than the man's own, and he finished his sandwich. He then said he was going to the lavatory and went into the yard. We never saw him again. Mr Pieters reacted very badly to the loss of his teeth and began to break the furniture apart, so I called the police.

Sex A La Carte

As a result of an early evening raid on the Bamboo Villa, a restaurant in the centre of Calcutta, in June 1990, Inspector Prasna Mukkerjee of the city's CID said his men had arrested a total of 36 people comprising 7 solicitors, 5 accountants, 2 insurance brokers and 22 women. In a statement to the *Calcutta Statesman*, he explained:

The Bamboo Villa is not a restaurant. It is a brothel. It does not sell food. Even very small snacks are unavailable. But it has fifty beds in the same number of cubicles. None of the ladies present had any experience of cooking or waitressing.

Snappy Request

When a retired merchant seaman, Pierre Cadious, decided to open a restaurant in Guidel, Brittany, he was determined that the lobsters he served would be the star item on his menu. But, according to a report in the *People* in

100

October 1969, he worried they might not arrive fresh enough and set up a special arrangement with his wholesaler:

M. Cadious sends his order for lobsters by semaphore. He made this arrangement with the supplier – also an ex-naval man – because, he says, 'The French telephone system is so bad.'

Dinner Bites Diner – 1

Another French restaurateur in Paris who was also proud of his lobster dishes ran into problems when a customer complained that the crustacean paraded for his approval was not fresh. Angrily, the proprietor waved the lobster under the man's nose and urged him to smell it. But the story did not end there, according to a report of the subsequent court case in *France Soir* in July 1973:

With well-judged precision, the denizen of the deep reached out a claw and seized the tip of the customer's nose. Nor would it let go until it had drawn blood or (as one report suggests) actually removed the extremity of the (to it) intrusive organ, thereby causing the plaintiff pain and suffering and necessitating an operation by a distinguished plastic surgeon. The court found against the restaurateur and ordered him to pay damages and a fine totalling 250 Francs.

Dinner Bites Diner – 2

An even more remarkable instance of fishy revenge occurred in Hong Kong in March 2001, reported by the *Malaysian Star*:

Gourmet Tsang Kin-keung left two live piranha fish on the floor of his restaurant to die after buying them at a market. But when he picked one up to prepare it, the fish bit his finger. He was taken to hospital for treatment.

Owner Bites Dog

Newspapers rarely show much interest in stories about dogs biting people unless, of course, one or the other happens to be famous. When the reverse is true, though, reporters will snap furiously to get the tastiest details, as this cutting from the *News of the World* in 1987 demonstrates:

The owner of Langan's Brasserie in London, Peter Langan, scuttled across the restaurant floor on all fours and bit the hind leg of a small dog belonging to the Italian clothes designer, Elio Fiorucci.

Langan is, of course, famous for outlandish exploits in his London restaurant, which have earned him the accolade of 'Cuisine's answer to Brendan Behan'. In 1989 the *Sunday Times* listed a few:

He has offered female customers unlimited champagne to strip off; taken off his shoes and dumped them on a lady's plate before coyly settling himself in her lap; and swallowed a cockroach.

Kicking Up A Fuss

When the smart new Bancroft Hotel in Saginaw, Michigan, opened its doors in 1879, the owner decided to host a grand opening banquet to which he invited all the local dignitaries and wealthy businessmen. Unfortunately, he forgot to invite the millionaire Curt Emerson, a man famous for his temper and eccentricity. A report in the *Detroit Free Press* the following day noted:

Just as the guests began tucking into Terrapin a la Maryland, *Mr Emerson suddenly appeared, leapt screaming on to the long table and kicked his way from one end to the other, sending dishes and guests flying. Today, we understand, he has paid the hotel $2000 compensation, and the proprietors have confirmed that he will never be omitted from a guest list again.*

The Gravy Train

Another American millionaire, the newspaperman James Gordon Bennett, who founded the London and Paris editions of the *New York Herald*, was a man who enjoyed creating headline-grabbing stunts. He became the centre of one in 1912 when he walked into his favourite restaurant in Monaco and found every table occupied. His obituary written by the *Herald* in 1918 tells the outcome:

> *Bennett was so annoyed to find the restaurant full that he promptly bought the premises from the owner and had the other diners escorted out of the building. He then sat down for his usual meal of seven well-done mutton chops with pints of thick, lamb-fat gravy. After the meal, his appetite satisfied and his good humour restored, Bennett summoned the former owner. He presented the man with the bill of sale of the restaurant and said, 'The restaurant is yours to keep. The only condition is that you will always serve me with as many mutton chops and gravy as I require at any time of the night or day!'*

Poulet A La Mode

That wise old saying of chefs that 'Mayonnaise can hide a multitude of things' was perhaps most bizarrely illustrated in Italy in April 1938. A report in *The Times* explained the strange story of a man from Milan who ordered a dinner for himself and six friends at a leading restaurant:

> *He then lay down on the table, covered his face with mayonnaise sauce, and said to a somewhat startled waiter, 'Carve me just like a chicken.' He was rushed to hospital and explained that he had been crossed in love.*

Object No Expense

As Jonathan Willis walked into the Minstrel Restaurant in Bournemouth in August 1985 he gave every indication of being a good customer. The *Bournemouth Evening Echo* reported that he ate a four-course meal, drank two bottles of wine and, over two glasses of brandy, smoked an expensive cigar. Willis then asked a waiter if he could use one of the Minstrel's 'At-Your-Own-Table' telephones:

Given the phone, Mr Willis called the local police and told them as he could not pay his bill, they should come and arrest him. He explained, 'I have been unemployed for sixteen years and felt in need of a treat.'

Flushed With Anger

James Tucker was far from happy with the dish of chicken curry which he ate at the Diamond Restaurant in St Hellier in October 1979. In fact, he left the restaurant without paying and later appeared in court, a report in the *Jersey Evening Post* stated. Tucker told the police:

I had over £20 in my pocket at the time, but the food was so disgusting that I flushed the money down the toilet rather than pay up.

Boiling Rage

The disturbance in the kitchens at Brasenose College, Oxford, in February 1980 startled all those within hearing distance and resulted in the following report in the *Daily Telegraph*:

Mr John Pawlec, a cook of 14 years standing, went berserk in the college kitchens and destroyed over £1,000 worth of kitchen equipment. He said he was astounded at being told he was boiling eggs in the wrong way.

There's A Fly In My Waiter!

The joke about the fly in the soup has been a favourite with cartoonists and comedians for many years. But a new variation on the old theme was reported from China in October 2000 in the Shanghai newspaper, *Wen Wei Pao*. The events occurred at the Hotel Toronto in Harbin Province and concerned two diners who demanded to see the chef when one of them found a fly in his soup. The chef apparently looked at the fly, picked it out of the dish with his fingers, and then ate it. The paper's account continued:

According to the general secretary of the Harbin Consumers' Association, this practice has been imposed in all the city's eating establishments, so that kitchen staff are more careful with food and hygiene. It is compulsory for staff to eat insects if they want to keep their jobs. If they do eat it, they get up to 500 yen for each fly they eat.

One Swallow Does Not Make A Meal

The night Idris Sathe, an accountant from Mysore, decided to take his wife out for supper to celebrate their wedding anniversary, he did not bargain for what she found on her plate. The *Deccan Herald* reported the incident when Sathe took the restaurant owner to court in March 1980 and told the magistrate:

When the idli was served, my wife noticed it contained a cockroach. She called my attention to it and I called the waiter. The waiter picked up the cockroach and, much to our surprise, popped it into his mouth, saying, 'This is not a cockroach, it is a delicious onion.'

Oyster Flap

Australian gourmet P.R. Watson loved oysters. He enjoyed nothing more than a plate of the delicacies – that is until the day in April 1986 when he found something quite disgusting in one shell and reacted violently, as a report of his subsequent appearance before the magistrates court in the *Adelaide Advertiser* stated. Fining Watson $250, the magistrate, Mr C.C. Vass told him:

To find a worm in your oysters is as annoying as it is to find a snail in a bottle of beer. However, you had eaten half the oysters before you complained to the manager. And because the manager required you to pay half for half, you did not have the right to butt him in the buttocks with the flat of your head as he walked away from your table.

A Slippery Case

San Diego housewife Nancy Tattoli enjoyed snails before a visit to the Limehouse Restaurant in Mission Bay Drive resulted in her instituting a claim for $150,000 in damages from the owner. The *Glendale Daily News* carried the details of the slippery case:

Mrs Tattoli claimed that one of the half-dozen snails she was eating crawled off her plate. Said her husband, 'My wife was so distressed that she fell down the restaurant stairs as she was leaving.'

The Bottom Draw

A quiet night out to dinner in a local restaurant was rudely interrupted for Jane Bristam and her husband when they went to the Cardinal's Choir in Shropshire in January 1988. The couple had specifically asked for a window table, Mrs Bristam later told the *Shropshire Star*, and they had just finished the soup course when she looked up:

There were two huge bare bottoms pressed against the glass. My exclamation caused my husband to look up and, as he did so, two more bottoms, both bare, joined the first pair. My husband, who is a sergeant in the police and a rugby player, got outside double-quick and arrested them all.

Snaky Complaint

A diner in a Philippines restaurant who mischievously complained about the cleanliness of the place had his bluff called, according to a story in the *Manila Daily Bulletin* in December 1985. George Cabaso, a retired optician, decided to treat himself to a five-course Christmas meal at the Golden Duck in Baguio. The paper continued:

Afterwards, Mr Cabaso made his way to the kitchens and dropped a snake into a tureen of fish soup before lodging a complaint about the restaurant's cleanliness. Challenged by Mr Doa Tui, the head waiter, Mr Cabaso removed the snake and swallowed it.

Rat Droppings

Finding a rat in a salad would upset most people. But when one was discovered in a meal being prepared at the headquarters of the Civic Help-At-Home Group in Fordingvale, Mrs Raymond Gladly had a delightful explanation for the investigators from the Social Services Committee, according to a report in the *Ross Gazette* in April 1987:

> *The rat did not fall through the ceiling, let alone into the salad. He merely looked through and, to those of us who were present, gave a smile of encouragement before moving on.*

Jelly Mixture

There was quite a furore in Bath when news leaked out in 1969 that flakes of rust had been found in dishes of jelly at the town's famous Pump Room. But it was the manner of their removal and the implications which agitated a meeting of the city council, reported in the *Western Daily Press*:

> *The story was told by Councillor Will Johns who said that the waitresses had used eyebrow tweezers to remove the flakes. He asked that in future the tweezers should be sterilized.*

Something Of A Stir

When two London girls, Barbara Wintle and her friend, Moira, visited the High Time restaurant in Docklands, to sample the *Beaujolais Nouveau* in November 1986, it was more than the wine which surprised them. According to Miss Wintle who was quoted by the *Sun*:

> *After the proprietor had poured our glassfuls, we noticed that the wine had a cloudy look and asked his opinion about this. Instead of giving this, he opened his flies, removed his penis, and popped it into my friend Moira's glass. Then he handed the glass to his wife, who sipped it and said, 'Delicious'.*

Convenience Bar

Unusual names for restaurants and bars are nothing new. A French restaurant in Barnet, London, was known as *L'Abattoir*; Stirling in Scotland has Sawney Beane's Pakora Bar and Balti House, commemorating the infamous local cannibal who ate unwary travellers; while in America the Alfred E. Packer Grill in the University of Colorado was popular with students until it was realised that Packer had been a Colorado prospector hung in 1874 for killing and eating five people. Sentencing Packer to death, the judge – a Democrat – is supposed to have said, 'There were only seven Democrats in Hinsdale County and you, Alfred E. Packer, you greedy son of a bitch, have eaten five of them!' Less offensive – though no less amusing – was the application by a Yorkshire entrepreneur to open a wine bar named 'W.C.'s'. The *Halifax Evening Courier* carried the following report in November 1984:

> *Commenting on the decision by Calderdale Development Services Committee to permit Mr Bob Flurry, a butcher,*

to convert Bull Green's public toilets into a wine bar to be known as 'W.C.'s', Councillor Eric Yeats said, 'I am opposed to the development because you never know when the toilets may be needed again and – although Mr Flurry has agreed to preserve three of the urinals for their historic value – the W.C.'s will have no access for the disabled.'

Get Stuffed!

Southern Australia was in uproar in the spring of 1981 when the joint proprietors of the Europa Restaurant in Hindmarsh applied to the local court for permission to rename their premises the 'Get Stuffed Restaurant'. The pair, Erika Bayliss and Kati Ugrica, claimed there were already restaurants using the name in Europe. However, this precedent was overruled by Judge R. Grubb who said he loved the English language, but would not alow the bawdiness of Chaucer and Shakespeare to be turned into the 'slyly salacious'. A report of the proceedings in the *Canberra Times* – which referred to the judge as one of South Australia's wittiest dispensers of justice – quoted his summing-up in denying the girls' request:

When these ladies say that they are referring only to the legitimate and innocent culinary concept of stuffing food, I say, 'Rot!' If that was the case, they would call their restaurant the 'Come In and Stuff Yourself'. The fact that their friends and customers have found the new name 'hilarious' and 'terrific' cuts no ice with me. However, provided others agree, I will allow them to rename their

*establishment, 'The Get F****** Restaurant'.*
[The restaurant was renamed 'Fatty's']

The Bald Facts

Gimmicks are, of course, always being used by restaurant proprietors to attract custom. Sometimes they can misfire, though, as in the case of the Stage Deli in Manhattan, which decided in January 2001 to rename its chicken and bacon sandwich after the actress Kim Basinger. What the manager apparently did not know was that she is a leading *animal welfare activist*. Perhaps more likely to succeed was the scheme by a sandwich shop, the Neptune Subs, in Houston, Texas, to offer cheap meals to bald customers. A report in the *Houston Post* of November 2000 tells the story:

> *On the first Monday of every month – dubbed Bald Monday – anybody who is bald or losing hair gets a discount. Says Vinny Schillaci, the owner, 'If you're like me, it would be about 65 per cent off. If totally bald, then it's free. The more you shine, the cheaper you dine.'*

The Hole Story

Restaurants are not the easiest places to rob – but a few have been the target of inept villains. In 1990, for example, the Domino Pizza Restaurant in Balch Springs, Texas, was held up by a robber brandishing a *snapping turtle*. Two years later, a young man in Berlin attempted to rob a café with a *frankfurter in a bun*. Even more ridiculous was the exploit of Californian Harry Leone who entered a doughnut bar in Oakland in 1975 brandishing a gun and wearing a pillowcase over his head. Describing the subsequent events, the *Oakland Tribune* could hardly restrain itself:

> *Leone's first big mistake: he had forgotten to cut eyeholes in his hood. Second, one of the patrons recognised him when he lifted the pillowcase to see what he was doing. The cops were called and apprehended Leone.*

The Naked City

When the owners of the Tottenville Inn in New York found their stock mysteriously disappearing, video cameras were installed to catch the culprit. The truth proved hard to swallow, according to a report in the *New York Post* in February 2000, for the guilty party turned out to be the landlord, Albert Hohman, who lived on the floor above the restaurant. But that wasn't all, a spokesman told the press:

> *He was naked the whole time. We saw him walking around after hours eating meals. He even went behind the bar and made himself drinks.*

Blown Away

Diners at a restaurant in the centre of Toronto were horrified when a man set himself on fire in February 1973. The *Toronto Globe & Mail* carried a report on the incident, stating that the man was now in a critical condition in hospital, adding:

Witnesses said the man had doused himself with solvent outside and entered the restaurant because the wind kept blowing his lighter out.

A Rare Wigging

An important business lunch went awfully wrong for Mary Rollins when she was dining at the Sunshine Hotel Restaurant in Iowa in January 1979. According to a report in the *Des Moines Daily Register*, she was seeking damages from the establishment for the loss of her brunette wig. Miss Rollins told the newspaper:

I ordered a steak Diane and the waiter allowed the flambeau cooker to get out of hand. He snatched the wig from my head and poured a '72 Chateau D'Estephe over it. When it failed to go out he, plus two other men, stamped it into the carpet.

Picking Time

The bad habits of waiters and waitresses have generated innumerable complaints in restaurants all over the world. Probably the most apt words on the subject were delivered by the comedian Barry Humphreys, via his alter ego, the Australian 'cultural attaché' and gourmet supreme, Les Patterson, in 1998:

What can I get you this evening?
Said the waiter whilst picking his nose.
I'll have two boiled eggs, you bastard;
You can't get your fingers in those.

Gripe Page

Of course, the boot can be on the other foot when waiters and waitresses are subjected to unreasonable complaints from customers. For some years, the Internet has had its famous *Waitressing Gripe Page* with sections on 'Stupid Questions Asked by Customers' and 'More Stupid Questions Asked by Customers', which can be found at: **http://members.aol.com/GMAGates.** Television, too, has shown up both sides of the coin in programmes like *Restaurants from Hell* where a London chef was caught by cameras spitting on a plate of nachos before dispatching them to the diner, a Paris chef was seen serving a beer mat in batter to a man who complained about the veal, and an

American waitress picked her nose into the coffee cup of a customer who she considered a poor tipper. But those who work in the industry say there is nothing like instant revenge – as George Benslowe, the manager of the Golden Grape Restaurant in Bingley, Yorkshire, decided in December 1985 when a customer, Donald Walton, complained that his chicken was underdone. Reporting the subsequent court case when Walton was charged with throwing tableware across the restaurant, the *Yorkshire Post* stated:

Hearing the waiter say, 'The chicken looks fine to me,' Mr Walton asked to see the manager, Mr Benslow, who, on reaching the table, picked up the chicken, took a couple of bites out of it, and then put it back on Mr Walton's plate, saying: 'Perfect. A lot better than you get at home.'

Scraps Of Comfort

The Back Home Buffet Restaurant in Ottawa boasted that its menu was intended to introduce customers to the delights of vegetarian cooking. That was until September 1983 when health inspectors visited the premises and declared it was serving *garbage* – literally. Charged before the local court, owner Guy Paquette's defence statement was published by the *Ottawa Citizen*:

Mr Paquette admitted that he and his staff supplied their kitchen with ingredients from dustbins. He explained, 'Our aim is to educate people about vegetarian cooking. We have been operating for eight years and our regular patrons rave about our meals.'

Gastronomic Fervour

The fare was found to be even more revolting at a French café, the Chez Bibi in Paris, when health inspectors visited the premises in October 2000. They emerged from the kitchen choking for breath and holding their noses, according to a report in *Paris-Presse*. After closing down Chez Bibi, food inspector Jean Micheton told the press:

We found ten stone of rotten crocodile, hedgehog and monkey meat as well as bags of putrid caterpillars. Most of this restaurant's customers are African. They eat this sort of stuff back home, but that is no reason for serving up inedible rubbish that only endangers the consumer's health.

Making A Meal Of It

The story of Dr Sebastian Tanner, a professional conservationist, who sought compensation for being unfairly dismissed in March 1980, made headline news in America because of its unusual culinary angle. His case was reported by the *Washington Post*, which described how Tanner had been asked to inspect The Clouds, a local restaurant, to check on whether they were serving an *hors d'oeuvre* consisting of Pennsylvania Rattlesnake. He stated:

Imagine my surprise when I saw my fellow conservationist and the leader of the Washington Conservationist Lobby, Interior Secretary James Wheelan, sitting at an adjacent table with a double portion of rattlesnake on his plate. I drew his attention to my presence and the next morning I was offered a job in the Philippines.

A Tempting Course

In Britain during the Second World War, food was rationed not only in the home but also in those restaurants that still managed to remain open. The story of the customer who tried to ask for more in a Chelsea restaurant in August 1942 was told by Major Alan Theisiger at a meeting of the Borough Council and reported in *The Times*:

While I was lunching, a man tried to persuade the owner to serve him an extra course 'off the ration'. The proprietor firmly refused, saying, 'You know, you have inspector written all over you.' The man replied, 'You are right. I am a Ministry of Food Inspector. How did you know?' I have to say that such conduct on the part of officials was damnable. I don't think that in order to get convictions, people should be tempted into crime. Those are the methods that prevail in Nazi Germany!

A Cereal Book

When John Cleese was asked to contribute a recipe to a celebrity cookbook being published to help Christian Aid, his response was very much in keeping, said a report in the London *Evening Standard* in November 2000. His instructions to the author Margaret Simpson read:

Buy a packet of cornflakes, add milk and then add basil as required.

The Curse of Fawlty

In 1987, during a campaign to improve standards in hotels and restaurants, the *Sunday Times* invited readers to send them details of any bad service they had received. One of the letters prompted memories of *Fawlty Towers* yet again:

Recently my husband and I stayed at a roadside hotel and restaurant in Devon. The service was very poor all round, so on returning home I wrote a letter of complaint to the owner, asking for an apology and some repayment. I received the following reply: 'Dear Mrs Booth, Get knotted. Yours sincerely ———'

5

Pick And Chews

No restaurant worth its salt ignores the power of advertising. Although the claims of some eateries should probably be taken with a pinch of that proverbial condiment, on occasions the management drop a real hot potato or two when it comes to praising their own virtues. Among my favourites are an English restaurant that claimed it was 'Where good food is an unexpected pleasure', the Spanish bar which stated 'If You Eat Here You Won't Get Better', a notice in an Italian delicatessen, 'Our Best is None Too Good', and a Pakistani diner alleged to have a sign: 'Eat Here – Allah carte'. Two from America are perhaps a bit more direct, but none the less amusing: 'If you like home cooking – stay home' stated one establishment in New York, while an intimate Italian restaurant in the heart of Chicago's Mafialand said, 'Complaints to the Chef can be Hazardous to your Health'. There was also apparently a sign not far from here which challenged, 'If you don't like Italian food you're anti-pasta'.

The press are no better when it comes to reporting on the catering profession: 'Chip Shop Owner Battered Man' was wrapped up in copies of the *Gateshead Post* in 1966; 'Queen Toasted by Amin', savoured the *Daily Telegraph* in 1979; and the *Ulster Commentary* reported appetisingly in 1988: 'Catering College Head Cooked For The Queen'. With these sort of titbits, should we wonder that there is a French café in Dinard that amuses its customers with a sign: 'Broken English Spoken Here'. In any event, here are some more succulent samples from notices and newspapers around the world to enjoy, beginning with the card seen outside a restaurant in Malta:

We will allow you to pick and chews.

Top Hang Out

Acapulco, the beautiful Mexican city on the Pacific coast, is just one place quoted as a source for an example of that most familiar of restaurant misprints: 'On gala nights the chef throws his best dishes and all water used in cooking has been personally passed by the manager.' One of the city's popular eateries, *La Hacienda*, also offered this little gem in a March 1981 advertisement:

Come to Enjoy us in our Spectacular La Hacienda
With Mariachis, Music Beautiful
Open Terrace and Air Conditioned Entrails

The High Kickers

Across the US border in San Antonio, Texas, a sign hung outside the Taberna Capri which tempted passers-by with the information:

Meal and drinks while you dance. After a show play performed by the most hallucinating group of diaphanous show girls.

Management Problems

A Greek restaurant that opened in New York in 1987 attempted to impress potential diners with an assurance that the food was of the very best and the service exemplary. A notice just inside the door stated:

Customers who consider
our waiters or waitresses uncivil
ought to see the manager

The Rules of Etiquette

Trying to keep the highest standards has not always been easy for restaurants, and on occasions proprietors have come up with a novel way of getting their message across. For example, in 1973 the Restaurant Excelsior in Montreal urged its patrons:

Please do not put your cigarette ash into the cups. Call a waiter and he will be pleased to pour your coffee into the ash tray.

At the bottom of a menu in the Golden Eagle Restaurant in Toronto during the seventies was printed the appeal:

This may be a take-away business, but please don't take away our menu cards!

An up-market diner in New York appealed to its patrons in 1977:

Etiquette is knowing which fingers to put in your mouth to whistle for the waiter.

Uplifting Words

A restaurant on 42nd Street in Manhattan amused many customers with a sign posted outside in 1998:

Smart shoes must be worn, Bras optional.

In England, a Cambridge printer made an amusing slip in preparing an advertisement for a local establishment during a musical festival:

Succatash Sandwich Bra
Supporting the Arts in Cambridge

Cheeky Portions

The China Palace in Hong Kong prided itself in its advertising for 'titillating the palate and satisfying the most demanding tastes'. In an advertising campaign run in the *Straits Times* in October 1977, the establishment claimed to employ one of Asia's top chefs, Mr Chow Kum Ming, a man of more than 30 years experience. Among his specialities were:

A favourite of Emperor Chien-Ling
LITTLE JUICY STEAMED BUMS

Animal Crackers

The Restaurant China in the centre of Athens was not well served by the typographical errors in an advertisement it placed in the *Athens News* in October 1980:

> *One of the best Chinese restaurants in the world*
> *Serving all types of Chinese Chefs.*
> *Specialities: Chinese See Food,*
> *Mashrooms with Bamboo,*
> *Been Sprouts and Peking Fuck.*

Shark Bait

During the height of the *Jaws* movie phenomenon in 1975, a London seafood restaurant adopted a novel advertising campaign. Under the familiar picture of a shark with its jaws wide open, the management had inserted the words:

Revenge yourself now! Eat fish.

This same year a London coffee shop in Soho posted a notice, 'Shoes are required to eat in this cafeteria'. Underneath a graffiti artist had scrawled:

Socks may eat wherever they want to!

126

Raising Expectations

A Thai food restaurant in London's Fulham Road was anxious to present itself as being at the forefront of new restaurants in the city in the sixties and placed an advertisement in the *Evening Standard* in July 1969 which concluded:

> *In addition to the regular list there are daily specialities: Thursday – Stewed Dick and Saturday – Nam Prick.*

Room For Manoeuvres

Readers of the *Malay Mail* must have been amused at the advertisement placed by Shepherds Banquet Hall in Lorong in April 1981, itemising its special facilities for catering for big parties under a heading which read:

LOOKING FOR A PLACE TO HOLD A FUCTION?

Irish Delight

The *Irish Post* was the medium through which the owners of a popular Dublin restaurant chose to advertise one of their special nights in October 1982:

Legging Off

In October 1983, the Bamboo Chop Suey House in Shrewsbury ran an advertisement in the *Shropshire Star* promoting its extended menu:

TO TAKE AWAY
Selected Hot Meals & Chinese Cooked Foot

The Country Manor restaurant in Surrey was also guilty of putting its foot into its mouth in a notice posted in 1985:

One of our chefs is available to barbecue T-bone steaks, beefburgers and sausages, with customers giving a hand if they wish.

LEVEE AND SUPPER
OF THE
MAMMOTH COD

ASSOCIATION.
AT GLIDDEN'S HOTEL, IN NEWPORT,
On Friday Eve., Feb'y 16th, 1855,
Your company, and Lady, is respectfully solicited.

Three's A Crowd

A restaurant with the enticing name *Menage a Trois* put this advertisement in the London *Evening Standard* in May 1983:

> *The* Menage a Trois *is pleased to announce that it is now open for*
> STARTERS AND PUDDINGS
> *(No Intercourse) on Sundays*

French Leave

In endeavouring to promote the attractions of France to passengers on their boats, Brittany Ferries proclaimed in *The Times* in January 2001:

> *Bistros and brassieres line up and welcome you to a continental way of life.*

Direct Action

Having made it safely to France in the face of such distractions, perhaps a smart little restaurant, *Le Petit Maison*, in the Dordogne, would make an ideal place to stop. Certainly, if a warning notice hanging by the front door in 1982 is anything to go by:

In the event of fire, avoiding panic, is to walk down the corridor and warm our waitresses.

A hotel in the south of France popular with English tourists may or may not have been altogether serious when this notice went up in 1985:

A sport jacket may be worn to dinner but no trousers.

Hot Spots

A number of Indian restaurants seem to have made something of a speciality dish of the mishap. A notice in a Blackpool curry house some years ago boasted: 'Our curries are so delicious you'll repeat often.' And an advertising leaflet distributed by the Thames Indian Cuisine in Kingston-upon-Thames in July 1985 claimed:

ONE VISIT IS ENOUGH TO MAKE YOU REGULAR

Hospitality Guaranteed

The Dewan-E-Khas Indian Restaurant in Trowbridge, Wiltshire, was highlighted by the *Chippenham & Corsham Star* in January 1987 with an invitation to visit:

An exotic Indian oasis where you can find excellent authentic Indian dishes in a friendly hospital atmosphere.

Another Indian restaurant in Birmingham amused its customers in 1968 with this sign:

Between 4pm and 7pm tea and snakes will be served.

Dying To Be Helpful

A printer's error also bedevilled the good intentions of Henekey's Steak Bar in Staines who devoted the month of May 1979 to supporting the local Mayor's Appeal to raise £45,000 towards the cost of a scanner for the King Edward VII Hospital in Windsor. A report of their good intentions was carried in the *Staines Informer*:

For every customer who dies in the bar during the month, 20p will be donated towards the fund.

Suggestions Welcomed

Cliff Michelmore, the British television broadcaster, was a great collector of misquotes and listed among his favourites these lines found in an Indian restaurant in Glasgow:

If your wife needs something to do, she should apply to our suggestive head porter, but all of our staff are courteous and to ladies too attentive.

Tough Decisions

The proprietor of the Hotel Monopol in Poznan in Poland had a similar problem with over-enthusiasm for his establishment in this leaflet handed out to British tourists in 1985:

When you dine at our restaurant you will have the feeling of being wafted up to heaven. As for the tripe à la polpetta *you will be singing its praises to your grand-children as you lie on your deathbed. Or maybe you will try a* Tenderloin à la Chateaubriand, *tough as a pine lath. Well, then, you break your teeth, and so, without teeth and hungry you go off to bed.*

Tart Remark

A café in Melbourne, Australia, well known for its coffee and pastry dishes, encouraged passers-by in the seventies with a sign that read 'A wide range of tarts are always on the premises'. However, a small village restaurant in the Swiss Alps went one better in 1986 with this announcement:

Do not leave without sampling the tart of this house. She is strongly recommended, especially when hot.

Tea Like Mother Make It

Spanish proprietors have long been aware of the British habit of drinking a cup of tea at four o'clock. For years an establishment in Malaga displayed a sign, 'We serve 4 o'clock tea at any time of the day or night', while another in Lloret claimed, 'We always serve tea in bag like mother'. A proprietor in Benidorm tried a slightly different approach to lure thirsty Brits:

Roll and Butter free. Our crumpet is extra.

Perhaps with thoughts of drunken lager louts in mind, a third establishment on the Costa del Sol added:

We serve smashed potatoes.

The Naked Truth

The Regency Hotel in Portsmouth placed this advertisement in a local weekly magazine in 1958 to entice new custom:

The decor is most elegant, the service impeccable, the food first class, and the band terrific. There is a small dance floor in the gallery for the undressed.

Rhythm And Booze

Duke's Place, a fashionable restaurant in Birmingham with its own discotheque, took space in the local edition of *What's On* in December 1980 for a similar kind of

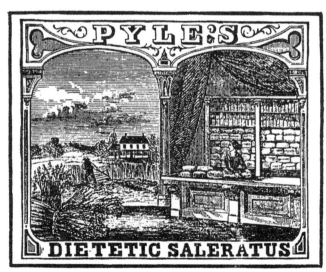

message. Until the printer took a hand, that is:

Delicious eating, Super Bars, 3 to be exact.
Serving everything from a slow comfortable screw to a glass of
beer.

The Sound Of His Organ

For years the restaurant in the Niugini Nivs Hotel in Papua, New Guinea, echoed to the gentle strains of music as guests enjoyed their evening meals. In August 1991, however, regular diners felt a mixture of amusement and embarrassment at a new notice posted in the foyer:

Wednesday, Thursday & Friday Evenings
In the Dining Room
UWE FOCK ENTERTAINS ON HIS ORGAN

Arousing Enterprise

As part of an advertising campaign in the sixties, the Palm Gardens restaurant in Detroit hired a vintage car and a man in evening dress to drive around the city drumming up custom. The poor man had one terrible lapse in his patter that became a legend:

Before or after the theatre, be sure to drop in to the Palm
Gardens for a pretail cockmeal.

135

A Pizza By Any Other Name

After making an equally terrible blunder in an advertisement for a fast-food establishment in Santa Barbara, California, in March 1980, the *Daily Californian* was forced to print this retraction on its front page:

The 'Greek Special' is a 'huge 18-inch pizza' and not a huge 18-inch penis as described in an ad for Blondie's Pizza. We apologise for any confusion Friday's ad may have caused.

Tongue In Cheek

The Ocean View snack-bar near West Palm Beach in Florida boasts an extensive menu of sandwiches all

described with degrees of good humour. A favourite with diners is:

Delightful Tongue Sandwiches. They speak for themselves.

Gestation Period

For some time in the sixties there was a sign outside a little restaurant in the Portuguese resort of Porto which read: 'Persons are neatly requested please not to occupy seats in this café without consummation.' A hotel in Bahrain improved on this in March 1979:

To Our Honourable Clients
NO CONSUMMATION TO BE SERVED
IN THE WAITING HALL

Behind With The Times

Emmanuel Marnieros and his two sons, Dimitri and Mihali, who ran a small restaurant in Kifissia in Greece, were well known in the eighties for their brochure which stated:

We have a staff carefully chocen – cooks, waiters and artists – will be occupied with you, in order clients to excellently serve. Our restaurant is idulic for great anus small and ideal for real relapse. Always you will find unforgotten moments of fun, amusements and danse on the pista.

Stirred And Shaken?

It would be difficult not to laugh at a claim printed in English in a bar in Tokyo which was on display for months before the *faux pas* was pointed out to the owner in 1987:

Special Cocktails for ladies with nuts.

The Wind Of Change

Another Japanese establishment in the same city, the Tsukuba Dai-ichi Hotel, also tried to lure tourists in an advertising campaign in March 2000 which proclaimed:

We promise you a variety of special foods in our comfartable restaurant.

Just for something to chew on, if you happen to be in Japan at any time, remember that the dish known as 'grilled eyeballs' is fried eggs with a drop of soy sauce, and to watch your table manners:

Do not use chopsticks as drumsticks to call waitress.

Service Included

In 1975 the Majestic Hotel in Istanbul put up several notices for visitors in French, German and English. This one hung outside the restaurant:

All our waiters have a course of instructions in European eating ways and customs so that they can do their best to serve you right.

Noises Off

A newly opened restaurant in Devon suffered from a newspaper misprint in the *North Devon Journal* of 1 April 2000 – and it was not intended as an April Fool joke, either:

With one fart of the restaurant set slightly to the side of the main eating area.

The county is also famous for its cream teas, of course, and one café proprietor in Teignmouth stuck a sign in his window:

Don't stand outside and look miserable. Come inside and be fed up.

Service With A Smile

Trying to make potential customers believe that a warm welcome awaits them inside any eatery is no easy matter. No doubt the proprietor who put this advertisement in the *Manchester Evening News* in April 1962 had the very best intentions:

> *If you really want Service with a Smile – Try the Marigold Self-Service Café!*

None For The Pot

Martin Shanahan, the manager of a fish restaurant in County Cork, thought he was in for a very profitable day in October 2000 when an American tourist walked in and ordered the entire contents of his lobster tank – forty crustaceans, all waiting to be cooked. What happened next totally astonished Shanahan, as he explained to *The Times*:

> *I thought he was throwing a party. But he took all the lobsters out of the restaurant and released them into the sea.*

Dishes Of The Day

The restaurants on Malta have something of a record for classic clangers. The Lavinia in Valletta offered an 'A la Crate Menu' while the Panorama in the same city claimed it was the place to come 'For a Nice Local Dish and English Food'. A small establishment in Mdina was on the same track with its notice: 'English food sold here – the breast in town'. The Mediterranean Bar on Gozo ran a promotional campaign in 1987 which read enticingly:

Fine food expertly served by waitresses in appetising forms

Getting Your Goat

The Goat Grill in Dar es Salaam specialises in just what it says according to an advertisement which appeared in the *Dar es Salaam Daily News* in March 1977. Under the headline: 'Goats! On a Special Occasion – Something Special Counts', the ad continued:

* *A goat for a cake on your wedding day counts.*
* *For a bite during parties, a goat counts.*
* *Enjoy with your family to slaughter and eat a goat on a weekend.*

Puffed Up With Pride

The 'Shots in the Dark' bar in Lagos, the capital of
Nigeria, has an unashamed policy of promoting its
attraction for tourists. This write-up appeared in *Discover
Lagos* in May 1990:

> *There is only one Canadian bar in Lagos and this is it!
> They specialise in shooters and are famous for their blow-
> jobs.*

The Daily Grind

Nice place, shame about the name is probably the right
phrase to describe the saloon bar in Oregon, USA, known
'Since 1932' as *Wanker's Corner*. But on the island of
Cyprus there is to be found:

> *The Bunch of Grapes Inn*
> *PISSOURI VILLAGE*
> *Fine Fayre*
> *Cold Ales – Clean Beds*
> *No Organ Grinders Allowed*

Among The Smalls

The unexpected is also to be found in the small ads in the press, too, as this selection of goodies will demonstrate:

ASSISTANT CATERING MANAGER/ESS. The applicant would have had experience of managing/ working with an extremely busy high-class restaurant/ coffee shop with the ability to prepare good food quickly and without taste. (*Walton & Weybridge Informer*)

BERNI INNS. The Exchange Restaurant requires a full-time Snake Waiter/Waitress. (*Evening Mail*)

CHEF. The successful applicant will be responsible to the Shit Supervisor. (*Caterer's Record*)

COOKER. Baby boiling. 2 plates, grill and oven. (*Edinburgh Evening News*)

DELICATESSEN. Learn a foreign language. Say: Liver Pate! Knackers! Bratwurst! Kasseler! Come and learn about other delicacies full of flavour and goodness from the NAS Delicatessen, Nairobi. (*Daily Nation*)

EXCELLENT SALARIES and benefits are offered along with marital status for Executive Chef. (*Caterer & Hotelkeeper*)

EXPERIENCED ASS COOK. Required for staff canteen. Permanent position. (*Torquay Herald Express*)

FIRE SALE. Eat here or we'll all be fired. (*Edmonton Journal*)

JOANNA'S RESTAURANT require a new line

assistant manager for our busy brassiere in Crystal Palace. (*Streatham & Lambeth Comet*)

LADY CHEF. Requires post; will go on hot plate. (*Yorkshire Evening Post*)

LOVE. Will trade my love for some good cooking. If good enough – matrimony! I am 50-year-old bachelor who likes fine food and weigh 310 pounds all from my love of good cooking. Write Sam's Coffee Pot, Riverdale, CA. (*Los Angeles Times*)

MEALS ON WHEELS. Trolley, elderly person never used in box. (*Birmingham Evening Mail*)

MIXING BOWL. Set designed to please a cook with round bottom for efficient beating. (*Beverage News*)

ODD-JOB MAN wanted to wash dishes and two waitresses. (*Glasgow Herald*)

OLD ESTABLISHED TUDOR TEA SHOP. For sale as going concern. Inglenook fireplace, masses of beams, low overheads. (*Catering Management*)

REQUIRED. Several staff to join our small friendly team. The shits are on a rota basis and can be flexible to suit. (*Garstang Courier*)

TWO COOKS. Required immediately for Winkfield Place Cookery College. Telephone Miss Grubb. (*The Times*)

WAITERS. Waiter/Waitress required as Marilyn Monroe look-alike. (*The Stage*)

WAITING STAFF. Exclusive businessmen's retreat for luncheon requires waiting staff to wear see-through blouse. Only refined young persons need apply. (*Adelaide Advertiser*)

WANTED. Full time cocks. £2.80 per hour. (*Warrington Guardian*)

WANTED. Preparer of food. Must be dependable,

like the food business, and be willing to get hands dirty. (*Irish Hotelier*)

WANTED. Up-to-date Gas Cooker suitable for single girl with enamelled sides. (*Yorkshire Post*)

WANTED IMMEDIATELY. Woman for Boiling Down. Apply Murray's Potted Meat Company. (*Auckland Star*)

WOMEN/GIRLS REQUIRED. Full and Part-Time for Crumpet Department. (*Cheltenham & District Shopping Weekly*)

L'Addition

And, finally, E.S. Turner, that great collector of unconsidered trifles from the world of advertising, reported this notice, which he found in a Paris restaurant, to *Punch* in October 1985:

Here fell J—— B——, where all is plush and gilded,
The oysters did not finish him.
The bill did.

6

Around The World
In 60 Menus

Robert Morley, the actor and gourmet, whose weekly column in *Punch* was always a fricassee of comic titbits and culinary asides, was a great collector of clangers. Those things that people say and wish they hadn't, not to mention the bricks that even the great and good can drop in the very best of circles. His book, *Robert Morley's Book of Bricks*, published in 1979, was a best-seller and there's no doubt that re-telling the stories has enlivened many a dinner party since – just as memories of his performances in *The Man Who Came to Dinner*, *Someone Is Killing The Great Chefs of Europe* and a lot of his other plays and films remain with those who saw them. Morley is also remembered for delivering one of the great gastronomic lines: 'No man is lonely while eating spaghetti.'

In his *Punch* column, Morley referred to several mangled menus he had come across during the course of his travels: examples of the handiwork of hapless foreign restaurateurs desperate to attract English-speaking tourists but less than adept with their translations. What Morley found, though, was only the tip of the *mélange* and he would doubtless have chuckled over many of the sixty examples reprinted in this section. But to begin with – and just to be fair to all those proprietors in far-flung places – I've included a few typical examples from much closer to home, where there really *is* no excuse:

Today's Special – Marconi au gratin. (Menu in Canterbury, Kent, March 1955)

Curried eggs filled with a delicate curried mouse.
(Advertisement in *Harrogate Advertiser*, 1963)
Rainbow Trout stuffed with muscles. (Menu in Bognor Regis hotel, 1969)
Stewed teak and potatoes. (Menu in London café, May 1974)
This Week's Speciality: Mules Marinere. (Restaurant advertisement in *Swindon Evening Advertiser*, October 1978)
Cheeseboard with Celery and Gropes. (Restaurant advertisement in *Somerset Standard*, August 1984)
We Use Only New Improved Natural Ingredients. (London restaurant sign, February 1989)
Grilled aborogine drizzled with chef's own pesto dressing. (Hotel menu in Lytham St Anne's, March 2000)
Our menu is guaranteed to wet your appetite. (Sign outside a café in Sudbury, Suffolk, February 2001)

Spanish Peccadilloes

Our gallery of *haute cuisine* spiced up in the translation just has to begin in Spain because that was where my idea for this anthology came to the boil. I spotted the following note some years ago on a menu card in a little restaurant in Madrid and the book – not to mention my stomach – was up and running (figuratively speaking, of course). Swallow what follows if you will!

When a dish has rum out of the Plate of the Day for ani circumstance the client will be entirely to choose any other dish for the some group of the card, even-thouth the said dish without surcharge being added to the price of the plate of the day.

Round the corner from this restaurant, tourists were being lured into another establishment which offered these main courses:

Salad with gardener
Rock Soup
Arm of a Gipsy
Saints Bones

That other lovely city, Barcelona, also provided two little gems. The first was in Las Ramblas:

Pork Loin with Jewess
Scrap-Heap Eggs

And the second, a short walk away, was even more varied:

Cocked garlic with mustard sauce
Marooned Duchess and Braised surprise
★

Bruined squid with pee
Baked Cheese Fingers
★

Cucumber Pudding
Live Fruit
Rhubard & Prune Surpise

On to Seville, where the girls and the oranges are so luscious:

Assaulted Artichoke

Eggs, Good Woman
Rape, Seamanlike Style

Valencia, too, provided an item to put any potential customer off the restaurant:

Breast of Foul Chef

In Madrid, there were shades of *Monty Python* at one restaurant offering the following dish:

Fried Brian

While at another, the amusement – if not the variety – was amazing:

Fizz soop
Whotes Dover (mixed)
*

Rost cock
Spited hen
Buff stek
Hambugger
*

Backed beas
Potato chops
Cabitch
*

Rice Sputnik
Pankasies with bebber & jem
Lemon jews
*

'Enjoy to eat now, always bring back after'
– Local mutto

In Burgos, it was the staff who suffered from the translator's error:

Noodle of Bologna
Brood of Eels
Tart of this House

On to the sun-soaked Costa del Sol where an establishment in Malaga got its excuses in first with this classic example:

Mus be comuest of tho disher, bread and win, one of the disher has to be meat, chikoen or fisk included breasd and wine or mineral water. The composition of this menu is expesificate in separe paper.

Down on the beach here, another management was more to the point:

Frozen Soup with Peccadilloes

And one more Spanish port of call, Marbella, for this selection:

Aside Rice Ham Fish
Crumbled Eggs with Tomato
*

Goose Barnacles
Natural Fish Knife (piece)
Gordon Blu
Thigh Lambskin
*

Pineapple Wirsh
Frost Pie

The Shrotted Pimps of Portugal

It is no great distance in miles or mistranslation to Oporto in Portugal where, a few years ago, a trendy little restaurant on the harbour-side tempted passers-by with these delights:

Shrimp Nets
Guttlefish
Squabs
Hen Blood Stew
Slop Brandy

Lisbon, too, has added its contribution to mangled menus with these delights to be savoured in a seafood café:

Shrotted Pimps
Boiled Frogfish
Drowned Squid

152

French Ribbing

Across the Pyrenees and into France where the *double entendre* can be a bit of a tradition in some areas. In Bordeaux, one establishment advertised a dish with something of an American flavour:

Extract of fowl, poached or sunside up.

In Nimes, a café made a bit of a foul-up on its main courses:

Young Partridge Over Sofa
Marseilles the Foot Package
Meat Between the Ribs to Trim

And even in Paris, which prides itself on being the culinary capital of the world, a restaurant near the city centre once boasted:

A Half Cock of the Countrywoman

A friend also assured me he saw the following *entrée*, although I have to admit that he is a bit of a joker:

Assiette Anglaise (Dishy Englishwoman)

Belgian Cod Peaces

Further north, in Belgium, an establishment on the outskirts of Brussels had a beautifully printed menu, stained only by these chokers:

Hand and eeg
Pissoles and reas
Frightened eegs
Sauceage eeg and chaps
Battered cod peaces
★

Roast apple tart and source
Biscuit cease
Cream Dognuts

A bistro in the same locality courteously informed its patrons:

All cocktails served with
cherry and small wooden prick

The Wurst of Germany

The Germans might not be noted for their sense of humour, but one restaurant in Gummersbach amused English tourists with this 'Dish of the Day':

154

Czardas Dish – Specialities Rich Garnished
For 2 Persons : Served Blazing

In Munich, diners with a night out on their minds might
have ended up a bit queasy if tempted by this offering:

Menu from 6 pm to 8pm
Worm meals will be served before the theatre

HOTEL DES BONS-ENFANTS

MENU

Cervelas - Langue fumée - Sardines
Matelote panachée au Vin rouge
Bœuf à la Mode froid en Terrine
Poulet froid
Sauce Rémoulade Campagnarde
Salade de Laitue rouge au Lard
Pâté de Veau et Jambon
Fraises à la Crème - Palmiers
Café à la Bohémienne

Austrian Mouses

Austria attracts thousands of British ski enthusiasts during the winter months, though not many would have chosen to sample this delicacy on offer in Kitzbuhel:

Fried mouses in vanilla sauce

Officials at the airport in Vienna were full of hot air when the error by the translator of this notice was pointed out to them in 1983:

Our most demanding passengers have discovered that a top chef has a finger in our delicious menu.

Swiss Whines

A restaurant in Berne, Switzerland, equally keen to blow its own trumpet only succeeded in blowing a raspberry with this announcement:

Our whines leave you nothing to hope for.

Swedish Surprise

The Scandinavians generally have an ability to master the English language, but the occasional slip-up does occur as in the case of this menu spotted in a Goteborg hotel restaurant:

Tongue Loaf with Leaves
Venison Parcel
★

Surprised Chicken
Craced Pudding (Biled)
Salami Stuff Roll
★

Rice Hashed
Mucked Shrimp

A Norwegian Pickle

In Norway, a restaurant on the outskirts of Oslo forgot to cross one 't' on a tourist menu and ended with:

Pickled Port or Boiled Rabbi

Much-Room In Finland

Further north still, in Finland, there was something of an international flavour about this menu reported in Turku:

Eggs with a Reindeer
Crained Pike-perch with Much-Rooms
Cock in Red Wine
Shanghai Sailors Chicke Curry

Polish Rashers

The Poles, too, have a way with words for the peckish diner. British tourists in Gdansk were promised by one restaurant:

Asparagus bunked in Ham
Smoking Salmon
Ham on Penis

In Warsaw, one proprietor's effusive language did not improve in translation:

Salad a firm's own make
Limpid Red Beet Soup
(With Cheesy Dumplings in the form of a finger)
Roast Duck let loose
Beef Rashers
(Beaten up in the country people's fashion)

But pride of place for the hardest-to-swallow dish must go to the establishment in the same city offering:

Boiled Stomachs

Czech Republic

An establishment in Prague offered on its 'Cold Toothsome' menu a 'slice of bread with fat and onion in accordance with your order' and:

Scrap from the Pear
Collared Herrings
Drowned Man

Hungary Dumlings

The Hungarians love their food and wine, but may have had some difficulty in getting their message across to English-speaking visitors to a couple of restaurants in Budapest. The first offered:

Jerked Meat
Fumigated Sausage
Fried Chinken
Dumlings Samlo Styl
Zingarakewers

Your guess is as good as mine about the last item. And it is not easy to make sense of these dishes from a second hotel-restaurant in the city:

Frogosh Miller's Wife Style
Fried Sheat-Fish with Spawned Cabbage
Noodled Loins in Bull's Blood
Robber's Meat
Spanish Bird
Dzrwed Boans with Pork Meat

Porn In Bulgaria

The beautiful city of Sofia has much to offer the visiting gourmet, though once again comedy found its way on to a menu:

Variety of Smoke
Strange Cheese

Another restaurant in the city seemingly did not give a second thought to what it was actually offering patrons who crossed the threshold:

Porn Shops
Bacon and Germs
Potatoes in Shirts

Yugoslavian Rags

The owner of a fine old restaurant in Postojna in Yugoslavia was for years asked for copies of the menu as souvenirs by British tourists, until one of them finally explained the joke to him:

Bismark with Hindrance
Clear Soup with Pancake Rags

The Gumpoes Of Greece

After Spain, Greece probably qualifies as the country which has provided the tastiest gaffes. Take this menu from a restaurant in Piraeus:

PETIZERS
Eggs of Fish Salat
BOILINGS
Head Half
Brains Salat
FISHES
Sfiris Fried
Porcies
Sguid Fried
BLUSHING
Lamp with Patry
Pof Coast

CHOPPED MEATS
Meats Ball
Bowels
Head Lamp
ON TIME
Geaps of Lamp Greece
Steks of Calf
Meats Ball Greele
OLIES
Gumpoes
Chick Peast
Beet Roots Garlic
CHEESE
Rok For

The four specialities of a restaurant in Athens probably raised eyebrows rather than expectations:

Suckling Ping
Beef and Heep Unixed
Lamb's Hers
Friend Pancakes

Much the same could be said about another establishment in the city:

Hoped Meat
Blight
Rice and Half Bullets
Tooth-Shell Baked
Utmost of Chicken as Hungarian
Lamb Smashed Pot
Thigh with Garlic
Bowels with Spit

Chicken's Liver Mad
Saussages Homelettes
Peaches in Tins

And perhaps trying to outdo the other two – unconsciously, no doubt – was this menu outside another restaurant within walking distance:

Little Joes of Jame
Warms Little Dogs
Combinated of Assaulted Greengroceries
Fillet of Backs Pig Cooked in Past
Fried Eggs in Torttle or Restless
Roasted Jame to the American Style

At Hydra, a bar tariff promised thirsty patrons:

Polls with Jams of Spoon
Tartars
French Lickers
Orange Tuice
Blandy Mary
Other Licferent Drings

And on Naxos, the gastric juices of any rugby player might well have been stirred by the invitation to sample this:

Lamb cook to a Peasant and Small Try

163

The Nipples Of Sicily

If Greece has not done for your taste buds, then give the menu outside a taverna on Sicily a chance:

Hen Soop
Consumate
Mellon and Prostitute Hams
★

Mukroni of Nipples
Spaghetti Fungus
Satiated Calamary
Red Mallet
★

Scallop Vale of Milan
Dreaded Veal Cutlets

SPECIALITY OF THE HOUSE:
Young Dear Hunter
with oberjeans, muchrooms and wite whine sorts
(All cocked up by your seat)
★

Raped Carrots
Groin Salid
Chipped Potatoz
★

Yogort and Gripes
Eyes Creme
Cofee Eggspress
SERVICE NOT COMPREHENDED

If such variety seemed a little too much, then there was always the speciality of a local Indian restaurant:

Stuffed Nuns

The Bowels Of Crete

On Crete the living is easy and the food delicious – if you can make head or tail of menus like this one:

Lamb Shops
Reddening Meat
Salad of a Village
Bowels Tomato Special

Farte In Cyprus

Another gem was to be seen on the Mediterranean island of Cyprus right in the heart of Nicosia:

Rissole of Lady's Thighs

For something a little less taxing on the imagination, a seaside café on the island offered:

Farte aux Fraises

Turkey Stuffing

A tasty dish of female anatomy was also to be found in nearby Turkey outside a restaurant in the centre of Istanbul:

Mixed girll with Baked Beings

In a café in the city of Ankara, English-speaking patrons were offered:

Stuffed Meat Copulate

A hotel in the same place no doubt had the best of intentions when putting up this notice:

You are invite to visit our restaurant where you can eat the Middle East foods in an European ambulance.

Perhaps the simplest thing was to go for a straightforward option in a fast-food establishment:

Tasteful Chicken in Paperbag

The Larks of Egypt

For some years, a luxury hotel in Cairo not far from the pyramids amused English-speaking tourists with a menu offering these titbits:

Prawn Cock and Tail
Frog Leagues
*

Muscles of Marines
Lobster Thermos
Fresh Caut Soul
*

Two peasants
Larks in the Spit
Wild Duck in Orang Sorts
*

Cock in Wine
Lioness Cutlet
Biftek Gordon Blue
*

French Beas
French Fried Ships

Sprouts of Bruxelles

★

Please to try the Tarts of this House
available for your delight on the trolley

★

If you are wishing to show feelings,
wait until you see the manageress

The same city also possessed another establishment which prided itself on one particular category of food:

FOUL DISHES
Foul with French Oil
Foul with Brown Beans
Foul with Dick

The Catstails Of Baghdad

Two establishments in Baghdad were well known among travellers for their amusing menus. The first, a café, boasted:

Pimps No 1 or Pimps No 2
Shrimps Catstails
Cram Chaps
Chateaubriana for 3 Parsons

The other, a hotel-restaurant, listed for the benefit of patrons:

Coloured Soop

Fish with Beas
Small Meat
Kari Hans with Rice
Hurts with Eggs & Potatoes
Bakred Mukroni
Sandwich Coloured
Pee with Milk
Vimto

Strongenuff In Thailand

The increasing number of Western tourists visiting Thailand has provided restaurants with a whole new range of customers – and every opportunity to mistranslate some popular dishes. This first menu was seen in Nakhon Ratchasima:

Testicles of Bull
Udder Milk Bag
Female Calf Intestine
Little Kids (Roasted or at Spit)
Apple Pancake burned with Rum

In the capital, Bangkok, invention had also run riot in a stylish new establishment:

Wedding Soup
Split Tummy Egg Plant
Nightingale Nest's Swet
Virgin Lips
Beef Strongenuff

Stewed Abalone with 3 Things
Fried Gut
Lucky Duck

A more modest establishment had this puzzling dish on offer:

Claypot with eight fairies

But a coffee shop in Chiang Mai managed better than the others, with just one crucial word going astray:

TODAY'S SPECIAL
Fried crispy wanton
– with beef & vegetables

Eastern Potlucks

With its long tradition of English-speaking residents and tourists, menus in Hong Kong are not now very often subject to boobs. However, this sign in the American Restaurant has been reprinted more than once in the US press:

Will-Known Menu Chinese & Western
Excellent Wines & Potlucks
Ordinary Meals of Your Own Accord
Pudding Specialists in Roast Chickens
Sanitary Equipments – Hospitable Waiters

And, finally, before serious indigestion sets in, a classic

dish from a restaurant menu in Singapore to remind one
and all of home:

Boiled Combinations

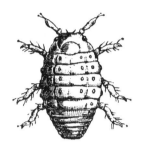

7

Pounds Of Flesh

In December 2000, two lecturers at Imperial College in Ashford, Kent, told their students to eat worms. The doctors, Nigel Poole and Andrew Dorward, opened more than just a can of the wriggly creatures when they asked the young men and women to augment their diets with the mopane worm, which is considered a delicacy in its native Botswana, Zimbabwe and South Africa. The pair of academics had been awarded a £500,000 grant to study the worm in order to help poor communities in those countries harvest it more efficiently and increase productivity. The foot-long worm is apparently collected, dried and exported for sale all year round. Explained Dr Poole, 'The mopane worm is important for millions in southern Africa – in terms of dry weight it's about 60 per cent protein so it's high in nutritive value. It is a bit rubbery and crunchy.' The experiment – and the students' reaction – naturally caught the appetite of the press and one of the female students delivered their verdict to reporters:

'They're disgusting. They don't taste of much and the texture's horrible.'

Worms are by no stretch of the human digestive organs the strangest dish to have been set before kings or commoners. Nor have some men and women been as reluctant as the Imperial College students to dine on the extraordinary, the unlikely and the plain bizarre. Indeed, there is even a word, *pica*, which describes the desire to eat odd things – especially dirt, hair and clay. So take your pica of some of the weird tastes collected for your delectation in this section – *if* you have the stomach for it . . .

A Lot Of Garbage

The word garbage has actually been used to describe bad meals for a very long time – although back in the Middle Ages there was a recipe for Garbage which was nowhere near as bad as it sounds. Historian James Solheim, who has tracked down the recipes for such medieval favourites as Roast Cockatrice (a mythical creature half pig and half chicken) and Boiled Flamingo (scalded with its feathers on, apparently, and stuffed with celery), recently translated the ancient formula into modern English:

Take good garbage (chickens' heads, feet, livers and gizzards) and wash them clean. Place in a clean pot and add fresh broth of beef, powder of pepper, cinnamon, cloves, mace, parsley and sage minced small. Then take some bread, steep it in the same broth, draw it through a strainer, and throw it in the pot and allow to boil. Add powdered ginger, grape juice, salt and a little saffron and serve.

Blackbird Pie

In the sixteenth century, wild birds were often caught for food. Dumplings stuffed with sparrows or larks graced many a table, and thrushes and blackbirds were also popular fare with country people. The Welsh especially liked 'Pickled Puffin'. One dish known as 'Revelry Pie' inspired the famous nursery rhyme, 'Sing a Song of Sixpence', with its 'Four and Twenty Blackbirds Baked in a Pie' and a description written in 1625 explains just why:

The pie of coarse pastry is baked first, then allowed to cool, after which birds (sometimes frogs) are pushed in through holes in the bottom of the crust. Their fluttering (or jumping) to freedom when the pie is cut open causes much delight and pleasure to the whole company.

Rat, Anyone?

Although the very idea of eating rats may seem revolting, gourmets in the past claimed that a fat rat, well cooked, was not bad at all. Indeed, there are recipes for roasted rat with breadcrumb-and-herb stuffing, as well as grilled with oil and shallot sauce. Rat pie was popular in England for many years, although the folk in the Philippines prefer rat-meat sausages. But it is the Chinese who have the longest tradition of catching field rats and cooking them fresh-killed or dried. The following delicacies are said to still be popular in some country districts:

Crispy fried rat with lemon
Boiled bamboo rat
Roast rat with desiccated deer's penis

Muddy Flavour

In the deep south of America there is a tradition of eating mud – which has nothing to do with the delicious chocolate pie. The custom has been recorded among the cotton pickers in the Mississippi Delta, where some hardened mud-eaters have had to be weaned off the diet with baking soda or starch. A report in the *Louisville Times* in April 1994 quoted Mrs Fannie Glass, who said her family had been eating mud for generations:

It's after the rainfall when the earth smells so rich and flavourful that mud is best. I eat it either on its own or seasoned with salt and vinegar in a pie.

Getting In A Stew

Mud also featured in a divorce case brought by Robert Wate of Paterson, New Jersey, against his wife, Edna, in March 1955. Their acrimonious marriage was described in a report by the *Paterson Evening News* which quoted the husband's grounds:

I brought my boss home to dinner for the first time and what did she do? She served this stew made of chunks of mud, chopped lamb and a fried automobile tire.

A Prickly Dilemma

A husband who threatened his wife unless she ate an equally curious dish was the subject of a divorce case at Leicester Court in June 1964. Jill Bennet alleged cruelty against her husband who said he would cut off her head unless she ate some hedgehog which he had prepared for supper. According to a report in the *Daily Mirror*, she ate some but refused to clear her plate. Arthur Bennet told the court:

In Buckinghamshire hedgehog is considered a favourite dish. I made her eat half so that her big, ugly sister should not have it.

A Heartily Shocking Appetite

The nineteenth century geologist William Buckland had rocks in his head where eating was concerned. When he was not deep in the study of mineralogy, he loved grotesque meals, according to a biography written in 1894 by his daughter, Mary. Buckland encouraged his friends to share his bizarre tastes, and guests at his home in Oxford were never quite sure what supper might bring. Toasted moles were offered on one famous occasion – which

Buckland declared were the most unpleasant things he had eaten . . . until he tried bluebottles. On another occasion guests were given a plate of soup and challenged to identify the main ingredient. Not surprisingly, several stumbled from the room clutching their stomachs when told it was alligator meat. But all of these stories pale in comparison with the night Buckland was shown a snuff box, inside which was said to be the heart of King Louis XIV of France. Mary Buckland reports what happened next:

'I have eaten some strange things,' said the professor, 'but never the heart of a king.' So saying, he swallowed it.

Buckland's son, Francis, also shared his father's palate and, after serving mice on toast to students at Oxford, developed a taste for boiled elephant's trunk, rhinoceros pie, grilled panther and fried slices of porpoise head. His *pièce de résistance*, though, was the spread he laid on for the Society for the Acclimatization of Animals in the United Kingdom – which he himself founded – at Oxford in 1862:

Slug soup with earwigs
Japanese trepan sea slug
Steamed & Boiled Kangaroo
Roasted Parrot
Leperine

Sock It To Me!

During the Second World War, some pretty peculiar dishes were set before the malnourished population. But nothing stranger than the dish reported by the *Evening News* in September 1943:

> *To win a bet, a soldier at Hadlow, Kent, fried a pair of clean woollen socks in a public house and ate them.*

And Pants To Him

In March 1994, Renato Arganza, a Philippines fisherman, was rescued after several days of clinging to a buoy far out to sea. He told rescuers his boat had capsized in a storm and only one thing had saved him from starvation. The *Philippines Free Press* in Manila revealed just what:

> *Arganza explained that he had survived by eating his underpants.*

Pregnant With Ideas

The bizarre items of food craved by pregnant women would almost fill a book on their own. The desire for nutrients or emotional comfort which leads women to try the most extraordinary things has been observed by doctors for years. Among the many theories advanced by members of the medical profession about this, is that the subconscious association of certain foods with times when the mother-to-be was happy or sad, and she then craves or avoids them accordingly. But just try drawing *any* kind of conclusion from these half-dozen classic instances:

* *In 1950, Elsie Martin, a teacher in Lichfield, Staffordshire, drank all the inkwells in her classroom dry.*
* *While she was pregnant in 1956, Pat Lemon of Kings Lynn fancied toilet paper and sucked it all day long.*
* *During her confinement in 1965, Sammy Butler of Brighton grew addicted to eating handfuls of rubble from building sites.*
* *The passion of Margaret Hunter of Exeter while she was expecting twins in 1976 was to take bites out of bath sponges.*
* *It was hot-water bottles and pencil rubbers that fed the appetite of Veronica Wise of London during her pregnancy in 1980.*
* *And the one thing that Judith Palmer of Birmingham found irresistible while she awaited her first child in 1998 was the taste of gym shoes – the smellier the better.*

Mental Indigestion

Although Canadian housewife Jeanne Willingham of Alberta was not pregnant at the time, she did develop a passion for a very strange diet. So much so, that in 1978 she was diagnosed by her doctor as suffering from a rare type of poisoning. A report in the *Calgary Herald* said the GP had finally pinpointed the cause as a specific type of mercury used only in paper-making. What *had* she been eating, he asked. Mrs Willingham's reply made news across the country:

I guess I've been eating the same things each day for about twelve years. A box of tissues some days, a cigarette pack on others, and even a whole paperback novel sometimes.

Cat's Milk

A reader of the Irish newspaper, the *Sunday Tribune*, disclosed her passion for a curious drink in a letter to the editor in June 1986. Helen Lucy Burke wrote:

As a child I milked the family cat and found the milk delicious – sweet and thick like cream with sugar in it. I got mouthfuls of fur at first, before I hit on the trick of squeezing the nipple into a silver teaspoon.

Dogs' Tales

Dogs have been eaten by people for centuries all over the world. The Mexican hairless dog was a prime food source for the Aztecs, for instance, and *Hon tsao go zo* is a classic Chinese dish, Red Cooked Dog. The Chinese also like the meat of the giant St Bernard dog, which is usually prepared with soy sauce or oyster sauce, while in Hawaii the people grill canines on the barbecue with sweet potatoes. An American academic, Florence E. Baer of the San Joaquin Delta College in California, even made a detailed study, *Orientals Eating Dogs*, in 1980, which provoked a variety of reactions across the country and the appearance of car bumper stickers reading, *Save a Dog – Eat a Refugee.* There were even more gross jokes and rumours of a new Vietnamese cookbook, *100 Ways to Wok Your Dog.* Eating pets may well be wrong, but one man who made his fortune from dog cuisine was a Nigerian chef, Union Agu, of Chukwek. Stories of how popular his restaurant, the Calabar Cross, had become were reported in the *Nigerian Daily Standard* in October 1986 with a quote from the cook himself:

> *Mostly we serve dog stew with corn and alulu spices or back chunks in pepper soup. Dog dishes are also getting special names. 'Gear Box', for example, means a whole head on a bed of rice with sweet potatoes; 'Wheels' means an order of legs with mixed vegetables.*

A Load Of Bull

While Paul Richardson was touring the nation to write his book, *Cornucopia: A Gastronomic Tour of Britain,* in the late nineties, he found a considerable number of exotic dishes ranging from haggis to a deep-fried Mars bar in batter. Only once was he defeated in identifying an item when he visited Bob's Tripe Stall in Accrington Market in Lancashire. He later told the *Daily Mail* in April 2000:

> *The most mysterious item of all was something called 'Dark Roll', a long tube of meat with a grey, spongy, ill-defined interior. What in God's name was it? 'Bull's wazzel,' said Bob.*

Yakkety-Bonk

The yak, that hairy, dumpy-looking beast, has become something of a delicacy in China recently. Mainly found in Tibet, where it has been highly prized for centuries, yak's milk makes a cheese that Chinese entrepreneurs believe could eventually outsell Brie, Stilton and Camembert. But according to a report in the *South China Morning Post* in November 2000, the cheese is not the only item of yak cuisine to covet:

> *Yak penis soup also has special qualities – it will endow lovers with enormous stamina.*

Getting The Hump And All

The *Guinness Book of Records*, which knows about such things, states that the largest item to be found on a menu anywhere in the world is *roast camel*. The animal's flesh is sometimes served at Bedouin wedding feasts and, according to a report in *Depeche Marocaine* of Tangier in 1994, the recipe is as follows:

> *Cooked eggs are first stuffed into fish. The fish is then stuffed into cooked chickens and the chickens inserted into a roast sheep. Finally, the sheep is stuffed into the camel and roasted.*

Cold Cuts

Eating people is also wrong, of course, but lots have done it. Ed Gein, the man from Wisconsin who wore the skin of some of his fifteen victims and inspired the films *Psycho* and *Silence of the Lambs*, is one of the most famous examples, along with Jeffrey Dahmer of Milwaukee who killed and ate seventeen people and kept the heart of one of them in a deep freeze. 'I was saving it for later,' he told the police. King Richard I apparently dined on the head of a curried Saracen and the former President of Uganda, Idi Amin, ate the liver of his foreign minister in the belief that

the man would not return to haunt him. Perhaps, though, the most bizarre account of cannibalism occurred in August 2000, reported in the *Sunday Times*. A Russian, Alexander Zapiantsev, was sentenced to 24 years solitary confinement after admitting to butchering a man and serving him up as veal at a banquet he threw for 20 of his friends at Chelyabinsk in the Ural Mountains. Zapiantsev explained:

He fell down drunk and died of cold. Why waste so much meat? It was very fresh.

Religious Tastes

That same year, Norberto Manero was released from prison in Manila after serving twelve years for having killed and eaten a priest, Father Tullio Favali. He told waiting reporters that he 'no longer had a taste for men of the cloth' because he had become a vegetarian while he was behind bars. In a statement to the *New Straits Times* in February 2000, he added:

People need not fear me, I am older and wiser now and I eat only cabbage and lentils. I am moving to the north because there are fewer priests there and I plan to open a restaurant. But as I am sworn off meat you can have full confidence in the wholesomeness of my cooking.

Gross Records

With the advent of a new century, the International Federation of Competitive Eating based in America published its first list of 'Gluttony Records'. This revealed that the Japanese, despite their diminutive stature, lead the world in 'Competitive Eating'. The fact also gave rise to a new theory, the 'Belt of Fat' concept, which postulates that large people are at a disadvantage when eating because their fat constricts the stomach. One previous holder of the fastest hot-dog eating record, Ed 'The Animal' Krachie, even submitted a paper on this theory to the *New England Journal of Medicine* but it was rejected. According to the rules of the Federation, published in the *New York Post*, sausages and buns eaten in record-breaking attempts may be gobbled separately – a method known as 'Japanesing' – and competitors may throw up during the contest – called 'Roman Style' – although very few do. At the time of publication, the world's fastest eaters are as follows:

BANANA – 24 in 12 minutes by Misao 'The Big Banana' Fujita, Japan.
CHINESE MEAT BUN – 4lb in 12 minutes by Takako Akasaka, Japan.
HAGGIS – One and a half pounds in one minute by Barry Noble, UK.
HOT DOG – 50 in 12 minutes by Takeru 'The Tidal Wave' Kobayashi, Japan.
JALAPENO PEPPERS – 175 jalapeños in one hour by Jed Donahue, USA.

JAPANESE DUMPLING – 117 in 12 minutes by Kazutoyo Arai, Japan.
MATZO BALLS – 12 in 5 minutes by Don 'Squirming' Leman, USA.
PIG SHANK – 6 shanks in 30 minutes by Marcus 'The Schnitzel' Steinhoff, USA.
SNAILS – 350 snails in 8 minutes 29 seconds by Thomas Greene, USA.

The World's Weirdest Recipes

It's pretty well impossible to list *everything* that mankind has swallowed. But here, drawn from sources all over the world, is a selection of the most bizarre and comical dishes on record:

APPETIZERS: Tarantula Dip, Fried Bugs, Slug Fritters, Froggy Croakettes, Coyote Droppings, Beetle Dip, Pickled Pigs' Ears, Jellied Moose Nose, and Lizard Tongues on Crackers.
SOUPS: Duck Blood Soup, Fruit Bat Soup, Iguana Soup, and Locust Bisque.
MAIN DISHES: Cockroach Stir-fry, Fried Beaver Tail, Beaver in Sour Cream, Crow Casserole, Barbecued Raccoon, Squirrel Squares, Seal Brain Fritters, Tuna Twinkie Souffle, Duck Webs in Oyster Sauce, Stuffed Moose Hearts, Moose Sukiyaki, Canadian Lynx Stew, Opossum Sausage, Curried Kangaroo Tail, Fried Cows Udder, Baked Seal Flippers, Fried Woodchuck, French Fried Skunk, Smothered Muskrat and Onions, Stuffed Squid with Chocolate Sauce, and Texas Rattlesnake.

DESSERTS: Garlic Ice Cream, Californian Spamoni Sorbet, Dirt Cake, Drunken Rum Cake, Kitty Litter Cake, Creepy Witch's Fingers, and Snowman's Balls.

An Ass Fit for a President

The North Korean ruler, Kim Jong II, was reported to have dined on roast donkey during his railway journey across Russia in August 2001. However, as the dish was considered a bid downmarket for the Stalinist 'Dear Leader', it was translated for his benefit as "Heavenly Cow," according to an account in the *Daily Telegraph*. The paper also reported that donkey had once been eaten at high table at Sidney Sussex College, Cambridge 1869, an event commemorated by a comic street ballad which ran:

Knifeum, forkum, feedum fun,
He haw! He haw! He haw hum,
How do you like your donkey done,
The wonderful donkey feeding!

8

Just Desserts

It's the nightmare every host or hostess dreads: the meal you spent days planning and then sweated over for hours cooking has come to a sticky ending. The fruit tart is just *too* tart, darling; the black forest gateau wouldn't tickle *anyone's* cherry; the whipped cream looks as if it needs a quick dose of SM; and the custard is not even worth throwing. When all should be sweetness and light (the pastry especially) once the starters and main course are safely under the belts of your guests, things can have a habit of going pear-shaped at the dessert stage. The cookery writer Faye Maschler put it very sweetly in an article for *A la Carte* magazine in October 1985:

4 Médailles d'Or

BISCUITS

DERNAUD

Le plus fin
et le plus réputé
des Desserts

EN VENTE PARTOUT

Pudding – the last hurdle of a dinner – is often the last thing you feel like making. The energy the whole event has consumed: the precision cutting of the julienne vegetables; the breath-holding over whether the mousse de fois de volaille *would unmould spotlessly; the terror that the lamb would be over-cooked or bright red and raw; it has all left you exhausted, dissipated and unwilling to vindicate yourself as a true British hostess by a flourish of puddings. A friend of mine told me her husband demands three: two of which must be hot and ice cream doesn't count.*

Sounds familiar? The dessert course can indeed be a hurdle, as many of the people in the following stories learned. And no cook should ever be smug, for even the best can end up eating their own words. Remember, too, that little kitchen homily:

Desserts spelt backwards is Stressed.

Chocs Away

Chocolate is, of course, one of the most popular ingredients of all in desserts. It was one of the staple dishes of the Aztecs – who thought it was good for the bowels – and, curiously, it is the only word of Aztec origin used regularly in the English language. It means 'bitter water'. The Aztecs used it also as currency: four dried cocoa beans would buy a pumpkin, ten a woman, while a slave cost one hundred. Christopher Columbus was responsible for bringing the first cocoa beans to Europe, but they took a while to gain popularity because they were originally served with herbs and pepper. It was the English who improved chocolate by adding milk in 1700, and almost three hundred years later – in 1986 – had to fight the European Community plan to rename it 'Vegolate'. Perhaps, though, the most curious story of all about this tastiest of sweets appeared in the *Observer* in October 1980:

> *Swiss federal counter-espionage agents have tracked down a young couple trying to sell chocolate secrets to foreign powers. They offered the recipes for forty different chocolates to the Soviet and Chinese embassies.*

The Great Plum Pudding War

Another strange dessert story took place just over a century ago during the Boer War in South Africa when a plum pudding was fired at British troops! The account of this culinary counterblast was dispatched by a Press Association reporter from Ladysmith on 29 December and reprinted in dozens of British newspapers including the *Eastern Daily Press*:

> *All is well here. The Boers have fired two plugged shells into the town 'With the Compliments of the Season' printed on them. One contained a piece of plum pudding. The enemy are still fortifying their position and are evidently determined to make a firm stand.*

Sweetly Made

Blackpool, the English coastal resort that has been a holiday favourite with families for a century and more, long prided itself on the quality of the puddings and desserts served in its hotels and boarding houses. A restaurant on the front had a notice in the front window which delighted generations of holiday-makers:

Try our Chocolate-Coconut Creams and furnish your mouth with the cheapest three-piece sweet in town.

A Snappy Morsel

There are lots of stories of people finding unexpected ingredients in their puddings. Take the instance of Mrs Joyce Maclellan of Glasgow, who was enjoying an apple pie with her family one evening in March 1956 when she suddenly felt something stick in her throat. According to a very deadpan report in the *Glasgow Evening Times*:

Mrs Maclellan put a finger into her mouth and pulled out an elastic garter. On taking the pie back to the shop her money was refunded.

Tastes Like Rubber

Pensioner Mrs Philomena Linkage of Ellesmere Port in Cheshire was even more surprised at what she found in a tub of cottage cheese in May 1985 – a condom. Explaining her amazement and her plans to sue the manufacturers for damages, Mrs Linkage told the *Liverpool Evening Press*:

> *I bought the cheese in a supermarket. One week later, while serving a meal to friends, I opened the tub and there it was. If I hadn't been careful I could have taken it in my mouth.*

Cake Decorations

The scantily clad girls who pop out of cakes at the end of all-male dinners have long been a tradition in America. This advertisement in the *Los Angeles Times* of 1961 is a classic:

> *Agent supplies 'Cake Cookies'. Pretty girls to jump out of giant cakes at stag parties. All our girls are attractive and fresh-looking. Fees inexpensive. Call Lou Plumb.*

However, being a popsy is not all sweetness and then light as an Italian girl found out in October 1995. A report of her fate was given in the *Corriere Della Sera*:

Stripper Gina Lalapola was found dead inside a cake she was supposed to leap from at a bachelor party in Cosenza. She had suffocated inside the chocolate cake and lay there for more than an hour before her death was discovered.

A Tale of Whoppers

Jennifer Year was not a stripper, but she did offer to dance topless at a charity supper party at the Good Companions Hotel in York in June 1987. The landlord then invited Jennifer to take part in a guess the weight competition with a difference, according to a report in the *York Advertiser*. The girl herself explained:

> *It's true that my 48-inch bust does attract interest, so when the landlord suggested a 'Guess-the-Weight-of-the-Whoppers' contest I agreed. As he produced the hotel's kitchen scales, a couple of old age pensioners in the audience collapsed from over-excitement. By the time they came around the scales had shown 4lb 3oz, but they both demanded a second opinion – so we let them have one. Everyone had a good evening and we raised £22 for charity.*

Buns In The Cupboard

The naked truth about a housewife whose buns got her into trouble was told by the *Sunday Express* in July 1978 – though the paper spared her blushes by not giving her name, although they revealed everything else. The young woman had just stripped off and was about to climb into a bath when she remembered she had left some muffins she was baking for dinner in the oven. Without stopping to dress, she hurried downstairs and, having removed the muffins, heard a knock at the door. Believing it would be the baker who usually called at this time of day and would come in and put her loaf on the table if she did not answer his knock, she stepped nimbly into the broom cupboard to hide until he had gone. The *Express* takes up the story:

A few moments later the back door opened and, from her hiding place, the woman heard footsteps coming towards the cupboard. The door opened and standing there was a gas company employee who had come to read the meter. 'Oh,' stammered the naked lady, 'I was expecting the baker.'

Frozen Sex For Supper

An unexpected sight also greeted housewife Rose Childs of Duxford near Cambridge when she took home an ice-cream gateau for her family's dessert in August 1979. A report in the *Cambridge Daily News* explained the subsequent events:

When she opened the box, SEX stared her in the face – in large white letters across the top of the gateau. When Mrs Childs asked the makers for an explanation, they apologised, gave her another gateau, and told her that the letters had been put there in a fit of pique by a worker who had been sacked.

Some Mouthfuls

It might be as well to avoid offering the following delicacies as desserts – unless your guests happen to have a good sense of humour. The country of origin is given after each item:

Bum's Biscuits (Sweden)
Grand Dick Wine (France)
Mukki Yoghurt (Italy)
Nora Knackers Biscuits (Norway)
Plopp Toffee Bars (Sweden)
Pschitt Lemonade (France)
Sor Bits Mints (Denmark)
Zit Fizzy Drink (Greece)

Self-Raising Physician

For years Doctor Ari Roga was a successful doctor in Salzburg, Austria. A tall, handsome man, he was noted for his charming manners – especially with the ladies – and he boasted also of being an excellent cook. In 1981, he was as good as his word and presented one of his patients with a beautifully decorated fancy cake. But rather than impressing the lady, he cooked his own goose as the *Salzburger Nachrichten* reported:

On receiving the cake, Miss M—— joked that he must

have had professional culinary training. Her innocent remark prompted an enquiry from another patient who had become suspicious of Doctor Roga and his manners. An investigation has revealed that he was not a doctor at all, but a pastry chef from Vienna.

After-Dinner Sweets

All Australia got a laugh out of the story about the restaurant which gave a new meaning to the idea of after-dinner sweets in 1990. The facts about the Fair Dinkum Restaurant in Perth were described in the *West Australian*:

The restaurant has been ordered by health officials to only use plates in future to serve dessert. It had invited diners to eat fruit salad and cream off the stomachs of its topless waitresses.

Slice Of Fantasy

When Phyllis Bayer, an 89-year-old grandmother, and the 5 other elderly ladies who had shared a birthday meal with her at her home in Adelaide, were rushed to hospital in January 1999, doctors diagnosed them all as suffering from acute narcotics poisoning. What had caused the problem was a cake bought from a local bakery containing a most unusual ingredient, the *Herald-Sun* of Melbourne reported. Mrs Bayer explained:

I love Mississippi Mudcake and when I saw one in the bakery window I went straight in and bought it to share with my friends. It was very moreish and I had three big slices along with my friends. The next thing I knew I was hurtling through the air, flying past the stars on a trip to the moon, with bluebirds and giant melons soaring past me as I floated upwards. I even saw Elvis, Harpo Marx and President Nixon. I'm telling you, I was completely out of it. I learned later that one of the employees had baked a very strong marijuana chocolate cake for a colleague as a birthday treat, but another worker didn't realise what was going on and sold the cake to me!

Gift From The Gods

Much the same thing happened to eleven firemen in Indiana in December 2000. A report in the *Indianapolis News* said the men from Elkhart had all had to be released from duty after a visitor left Christmas cakes and puddings at the station. The items were all laced with marijuana, and two of the fire crew had to be treated in hospital. Fire Chief Jerry Vaughan, told the *News*:

The fire-fighters are extremely upset that someone would do this. It just blows my mind.

Proof Of The Pudding

The case of Julie Wynn who successfully defended herself in a London court in August 2000 against a motoring offence on the grounds that she was 'driving under the influence of a whisky-soaked Christmas cake' provoked many reactions from the press and public. The best response, though, was undoubtedly from an unnamed AA spokesman who said, straight-faced:

I have heard people blame laced sherry trifle, but this is very unusual.

A Christmas pudding featured in another news item clipped from the *Fleet News* of Hampshire in January 1978:

Part-time firemen from Farnborough were called to a house in West Heath Road when Mrs Thelma Hall's Christmas pudding caught fire.

Patience Required

Hospital food has always been a subject of fierce debate – especially the number of choices that are available in certain establishments. Patients in the Middlesex Hospital, London, in 1981 were certainly offered some tempting desserts, but the trouble was ordering them. A report in *World Medicine* reprinted the menu:

Patients wishing to order Pancakes should tick the box marked Apple Flan and Custard and likewise patients ordering Jelly and Ice Cream should mark the Fruit Salad box.

Well Canned

The explosive story of the American cookbook that got a tasty dessert disastrously wrong was told in 1996 by *Reader's Digest*. The book – which was not named – contained a recipe for 'Silky Caramel Slices' and instructed cooks to put an unopened can of condensed milk in a pot and leave it in the oven for four hours. According to the *Digest*:

The publishers later recalled all the books at vast expanse when they realised they had just invented the first exploding pudding – they had completely forgotten to mention that the pot should first be filled with water.

When The Pie Was Opened

Less potentially dangerous was the misprint in an article in the *Financial Times* in November 1967 about the British and their love of afters. It stated:

Ice cream eaten at home now accounts for 29 per cent of the convenience dessert market. Such goodies as mouse and pie-fillings came out at 10 per cent.

Traffic Jam

Martin Gerard ran a pastry shop specialising in gateaux and sweet dishes in a crowded little street in Berne, Switzerland. Over the years, he grew increasingly frustrated at tourists who would park their vehicles in front of his premises. No amount of polite requests or admonitions had any effect and so, in November 1999, Martin perpetrated a messy revenge. It gave him satisfaction – but at a cost, as a report in the *Berner Tagblatt* stated:

The baker was fined 250 Swiss francs for covering the car of a tourist which he found parked in front of his delivery bay with an entire container of jam.

Tart Reaction

When two men held up a small restaurant in St Etienne in France they probably expected little resistance from the 64-year-old proprietress and her daughter. However, as *Le Figaro* reported in June 1986, they were in for a big surprise:

The robbers' demand for the takings was greeted with two large custard pies in the face, followed by a barrage of gateaux, lemon meringues and custard tarts. The aim of the two women was true and the robbers fled empty-handed, covered with food.

202

Getting Custardy

Bad actors and prevaricating politicians have also been subjected to the custard-pie routine. Bill Gates, the billionaire Microsoft founder, and Ann Widdecombe, the Conservative MP, are just two public figures who have fallen victim to pie attacks in recent years. Miss Widdecombe famously came face to face with a custard flan from the anarchist Biotic Baking Brigade in April 2000 and has probably been put off the sweet for life. Not so pensioners Edwin and Rose Freeman of Banbury in Oxford who the following month were given a year's free supply of custard, according to a report in *The Times*:

> *The couple claimed to have eaten custard every day for the past fifty years. Officials at Birds, the manufacturers, calculated that the Freemans had consumed 4,500 gallons since they were married in 1951. 'My wife's custard is just perfection,' Mr Freeman said.*

Cookie Language

If the British love their custard, then Americans are passionate about their cookies. So much so that the making of them can overheat even the most accomplished hostess. Take the story of the American actress, Marlo Thomas, berating her chef for having none when she is giving a meal for Gloria Steinem, which was reported by

Desmond Athol in *That Girl* (1986):

No f*****g cookies? I have guests who want cookies! Just what do you expect me to tell them? And You're supposed to be in charge! You go and tell my guests that you are so stupid you forgot the cookies!

Cookie angst even extends as far as the US military. When, years ago, the Chiefs-of-Staff drew up the US Army Regulations they even inserted a paragraph under the heading 'Regarding the Baking of Cookies':

The cookies shall be wholly intact, free from checks or cracks. They shall be tender and crisp, with an appetizing flavour, free from burnt or scorched flavour. They shall have been uniformly well baked with a colour ranging from not lighter than chip 27885, or darker than chip 13711. The colour comparison shall be made under sky daylight with objects held in such a way as to avoid specular refraction.

Mint Instructions

If that is all a bit hard to swallow, then how about the instructions given for making Mint Sugar Cookie in an article in *Gourmet Magazine* in July 1991. The error was noted by the Michigan newspaper, the *Ann Arbor News*, which reported:

One of the ingredients for the cookies that the magazine suggested was wintergreen oil, a toxin that can induce nausea, vomiting and in some cases death. Gourmet *was forced to send 750,000 letters in an attempt to correct the error.*

The Spell Of Desserts

As I mentioned earlier, desserts is only stressed spelt backwards – and here's a story to really prove it. It occurred while the sweet course was being served at a seminar in Toronto, Canada, and was reported by the city's newspaper, the *Globe & Mail*, in June 1985:

During dessert at a supper to end a ten-day Stress-Management Seminar at McMaster University, Mr Milan Gajic, a systems analyst, stabbed Mr Bob Kent, an accountant, with his table knife. 'He looked like a man who would steal your wallet,' said Mr Gajic.

Biting The Truth

And one last word on chocolate before we take leave of our just desserts. According to a report in *New Society* in January 1982, the kind of chocolate we eat gives away our deepest fillings:

> *Psychological research has shown that hard-centred chocolate bars tend to be eaten by people who externalise their worry when they are under stress. Soft-centred bars, however, tend to be chosen by people who can internalise their worries. This seems to bear out Professor E.H. Gombrich's theory that there are two distinct personality types: the 'biters' and the 'suckers'.*

9

Thinner Sanctum

It's been said that dieting is the curse of the eating classes. If it hasn't, then it should be – tastefully, of course. Now although trying to stay slim is usually thought to be a modern obsession, diets have actually been around for centuries. Records indicate that way back in the eleventh century, one of those clever Romans, a doctor at the School of Salerno apparently named Dame Trot, kept herself trim with the aid of friction rubs made of *cow dung dissolved in a fine wine.* The good lady said the secret of her slim figure was to remove all superfluous hair with quicklime, whiten the skin with leeches, and top the whole personality change off by rubbing the scalp with a mixture of *lizard boiled in olive oil*! Five hundred years on, figure-conscious Londoners were all chattering about the attractions of 'banting'. What this meant was they were taking the advice of William Banting, a former cabinet maker, who had become very concerned about his burgeoning girth. So he decided to cut out beer, potatoes, beans, milk, butter, soup and sugar, and eat only meat, fish and dry toast. When the previously chubby little man reappeared on the scene a shadow of his former self, 'banting' became all the rage! The Irish, you probably won't be surprised to hear, have a typically comic saying about the whole business of slimming: 'Talk about thin! Well, you're thin, and I'm thin, but she's as thin as both of us put together.'

Today, of course, hardly a week goes by without the announcement of some new super-diet. Many are forgotten as soon as the celebrity promoting them goes out of favour or the piles of cash she (or he) has made turn into pounds of flesh. There are those who claim that dieting is 'as easy as falling off a piece of cake' (to mix a metaphor), but most would probably accept that Skinny Mitchell's 'Weight-Watcher's Law' is more accurate: 'Better to throw it out, than throw it in.' The truth is that fighting the flab is a daunting business – and not without unexpected risks, as Californian John Ferwicz found back in 1953. When his wife, Mary, passed the 18-stone mark he decided to take drastic action. According to a later report in the *Los Angeles Times*, John quit his day job, handcuffed Mary, and then spent the next two years walking her across America in order to lose weight. *The Times* reports the finale:

Ferwicz's plan worked too well. His wife dropped to a trim 10 stone and she started catching the eyes of admirers as she passed. When the marathon finished, the slim-line Mrs Ferwicz left her husband for another man.

Expansion Plans

Americans are, by general consent, the most weight-conscious people in the world. Wherever you go in the States there are dozens of clubs and clinics advertising ways and means to get slim. No one from the big cheeses in Hollywood to the number crunchers in New York is immune. But serious though the whole business is, the occasional piece of unconscious humour does slip in – like this advertisement in the *New York Post* of 14 October 1965:

WEIGHT WATCHERS. Next Tuesday, 7pm, at the First Presbyterian Church. Please use the large double doors at the side entrance.

Pigging Out

The organisers of the Hi-Lo Tops Slimming Club in Oregon devised an ingenious way of trying to discourage members from sneaking snacks. According to a report in the Portland *Oregonian* in July 1975:

Any member who shows a gain in weight at the weekly check has to stand a large statue of a pig in their front garden for all to see.

Telling Porkies

Headlines in August 2000 claimed that American dieters had found a crackling new way to lose weight – by pigging out on pork scratchings. Thousands of health-conscious folks were apparently sprinkling them on salads, dipping them in sour cream or mashing them into a coating for fried chicken. One account in the British newspaper, the *Sun*, said nutrition experts claimed the high-protein nibbles stopped dieters getting fed up with tasteless diets. At the same time it was reported that an Englishman, Edward Burns, who had a fascination for the dried pork rinds, was carrying out an investigation into the various types. He wrote to *What's Brewing* magazine in December of that year appealing for help in his research from readers:

> *I would like to know if it was tough crackling or nice and crunchy with some soft fat bits. Did the skin contain stubble and traces of ink stamp lettering and was there much dried meat attached? There is no need to send full packets, unless the sender deems the product to be of such high quality that he would very much like yours truly to taste it. I am also considering a 'Campaign for Real Crackling'.*

Losing Pounds

A campaign to help lorry drivers in North Yorkshire lose weight may have lightened the load of some, but it took off far too many of the wrong kind of pounds for Ken Gray and his wife who ran the Copper Kettle Café near York. Appearing in court to give their reasons for declaring themselves bankrupt – a report in the *Yorkshire Post* of 6 November 1976 said – Mr Gray explained:

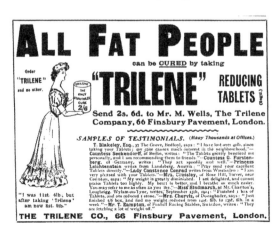

It was caused by this series of lectures on dieting. After that the long distance lorry drivers on whom we depended stopped eating lunch.

A Whiter Shade Of Slim

When Nuami Tambala, a pretty South African girl from Benoni in the Transvaal began a course of slimming pills in 1978 she was quite unprepared for the result. She had been suffering from a rare blood disease which had caused her to put on weight, a report in the *Rand Daily Mail* in May 1979 stated, which was why her doctor had put her on the pills. She told the newspaper:

I was absolutely horrified to find that the pills were not making me thinner but turning me white. People in these parts are very colour-conscious and I was terrified in case the Government reclassified me as white. When I walked down the street people would stare open-mouthed and say, 'Who is that attractive white girl?' Now I am on another pill and have almost returned to normal.

That Sinking Feeling

The members of the Wogga Wogga Weight Watchers' Club in Australia occasionally treated themselves to special outings as a reward for successful skirmishes in the battle of the bulge. In 1981, a group of the members set off for a trip to the coast. On the way, as needs must, they stopped to answer the call of nature. The *Canberra Times* later reported:

> *On entering a freshly tarred park lot, the bus carrying 28 members sank up to its axles.*

Memory Block

New diets are often featured in the press. Some of the methods are praised, others are questioned, but very few receive the kind of retraction that Starch Blockers did when it was mentioned in the American magazine, *People*, in June 1982. In the following issue of July 5, a paragraph by the editor apologised:

> *The June 28 issue carried a story on the new diet product called Starch Blockers. On re-checking his tapes, reporter David Sheff has found he misquoted Dr John Marshall. Dr Marshall did not say that the writer Cameron Stauth was a 'dirty rotten scum who got greedy'. What he said was: 'He's an unscrupulous little (pause) gentleman.'*

A Lot Of Hot Air

There was plenty of press attention in April 1985 when the British Department of Energy issued an impressive-looking five-page document all about dieting. One particular paragraph that caught the eye recommended that men who were on low-fat diets should wear thermal ties in order to prevent excessive heat loss. The significance of the day was not realised until a paragraph appeared the following day in the *Daily Mirror* of April 2:

> *The April Fool joke did not amuse everyone: Tory MP Anthony Beaumont-Dark complained, 'We do not expect this kind of thing from a Government Department.'*

Fishing For Success

Dietician Gordon Evans was a great believer in fish dishes for dieting. In March 1989, he wrote a feature article for the *Independent* about the results of a survey in various countries which made thought-provoking reading – until one unfortunate turn of phrase:

> *Spanish seafood is scarcely fattening. So you can indulge yourself without worrying about the scales.*

Brownie Points

The Duchess of York, whose battles with her weight have been regularly reported ever since her marriage to Prince Andrew, explained in an interview to the *Sunday Times* in December 2000 about how she involved her two daughters in counting calories. She told the newspaper:

They test my knowledge as in, 'Mummy, how many points for the two brownies you're just about to eat?'

Taking The Powder

An American diet fanatic spent years trying to find a form of nutrition that did not contain a single calorie. This he hoped would help him to lose weight and earn him a fortune when he marketed the product. A report on the man's endeavours appeared in an article on slimming in the *New York Mirror* in 1960:

Searching for a calorie-free food, he tried powdered glass, coal and sand before settling for chopped surgical cotton and fruit juice. He lost no weight.

Dogged Determination

Not quite so unappetising was the method of dieting that Joan Skinner of Devon passed on to readers of *Woman's Realm* in September 2000. Here success was all down to a neighbour's *dog*, she said:

I'd agreed to look after Henry for a month while his owners were away. He followed me everywhere. Each time I ate, he was there, staring intently at me. In the end he made me feel so guilty that I became determined to lose weight. I'm already 10lb lighter and if I ever feel tempted back to my old ways, I just think of Henry!

Belt-Up For Success

In November 1999, Italian professor Piero De Giancomo announced that he had finally invented the perfect solution for all those who were overweight – a modern-day version of the chastity belt. An account of the professor's work as the director of the impressively named Centre of Eating Habits Disturbances in Bari was given in the *Giornale D'Italia*:

The Cintura de Vastita, *or* Vastity Belt, *contains a microchip that senses when the belt is stretched beyond a certain limit. It flashes and beeps if the wearer has eaten too much.*

Ring Of Confidence

Linda Leiro, an English girl married to an Italian and living in Wimbourne, Dorset, was extremely conscientious about her diet, to the extent that she lost so much weight her wedding ring kept falling off her finger. Then when an advertisement with her phone number offering, 'Wedding Ring for sale – Hardly used' appeared in the *Dorset Evening Echo*, anxious relatives wondered if divorce was in the air. They were relieved to learn that Linda's husband, Alberto, had bought a new ring to replace the old one – but the story did not end there as the *Evening Echo* reported:

Linda had got fed up with her diet and took to eating biscuits, cream cakes and plates of pasta again. The weight rolled back on and so did the old wedding ring. It was the new one, now far too small, that Linda put up for sale.

Star Dishes

Among the many film and TV stars who have lent their names to diet books and slimming courses in recent years, two of the best known are Joan Collins and Shirley Maclaine – both of whom have suffered amusing newspapers misprints. Joan Collins was in the *Kettering & Corby Leader* in November 1983:

Dynasty star Joan Collins at 50 has a figure as slender as a girl's due, she says, to living mainly on salads, 'with just one main meal a day which is generally very lightly cooked fish or children'.

Shirley Maclaine suffered her bit of bad taste in a profile in *What Diet?* of all places:

Actress Shirley Maclaine might be past 50 but you've got to hand it to her – she still has more than her fair share of sex appeal. She looks and feels terrific and as she says herself, she has 'a lot to offer a man'.
Date of birth: 24.4.34. Height: 5' 6" Weight: 87st 5lb.

Breaking The Pound Barrier

Slimming clubs and diet centres love their slogans, especially puns. Here is a selection of the best that I have collected from all over the world:

A slimming clinic in the heart of London's fashionable Kensington:
Here today, gaunt tomorrow.
Outside a slimming clinic in Eastbourne, Sussex, is a placard:
Make sure you tip *our scales – don't* bribe *them.*
A restaurant in Manchester which specialises in slimming dishes:
Our dishes will take your breadth away.
From the door of a slimmer's club in Edinburgh, Scotland:
Waist Not, Want Not.

A Welsh slimming clinic proudly claimed in the seventies:

Stop here and break the pound barrier.

In the window of a Belfast slimming clinic were the words:

Tubby or not tubby, fat is the question.

A 'Reducing Clinic' in Winnipeg, Canada, still challenges clients:

Overweight? It could be just your desserts.

A sign outside a slimming clinic on New York's Wall Street:

Slimming for Stocky Brokers.

Another fitness salon in the Big Apple claims:

We will reduce your hips – or bust.

A ladies' slimming clinic in Boston, USA, announces over the door:

For the woman who is thick and tired.

A variation of this can be seen in a health-food clinic in Chicago:

Our diets are for people who are thick and tired of dieting.

Above the reception desk in a Miami slimming clinic:

Beware of the Noah Factor – Don't take Two of Everything.

A health farm in Brisbane, Australia, offers a guarantee to clients:

Two weeks with us will ensure that your end justifies the jeans!

Diet-Speak

Everyone knows that most of the claims made for diets don't mean exactly what they say. In February 1991, the *Daily Mail* offered readers an interpreter's guide which listed these half a dozen comic titbits:

Developed by Top Scientists – It's expensive.
Vitality Diet – Eat green salads.
Wonder Diet – Being investigated by the Department of Health.
Total Dieting System – Includes paper to keep a note of your weight.
Totally Natural – Drink Water.
Slimming Secrets – Eat Less.

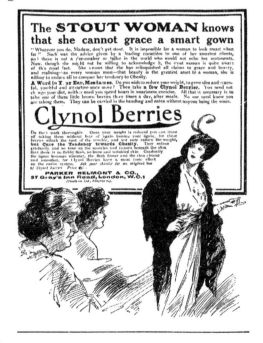

The Agony Column

To end on a salutary note. Readers have been writing to newspapers and magazines for years seeking advice on dieting. The majority are anxious to lose as many pounds as they can reasonably afford, but there are others who see it as a way of not eating and saving a bit of dough. Take heed of this letter to *Weekend* magazine in 1964:

For years my husband and I have been living on a diet of milk and biscuits and very little else in order to save money for a deposit on a house of our own. At last we have moved into the house of our dreams, but we are still living on the same diet. The strain of years of saving have given us both chronic stomach trouble.

10

Cooking Will Be The Death Of Me

There are some pretty strange statistics to be found in the world of cooking – and I don't just mean the sort of things that get boiled or basted or even the measurement of curious ingredients. Perhaps the most predictable is that while men tend to kill their wives in the bedroom, women favour the kitchen. It's also apparently true that the first four minutes a couple spend together at the breakfast table is likely to ignite an argument – and that excludes burning the toast. There's a perfect example of that, too: the Great Fire of London. It all started when Thomas Farriner and his wife were cooking bread in their home in Pudding Lane, London, on 2 September 1666. One cross word as their backs were turned and the oven caught fire. The result was a blaze that spread through the poky little buildings and narrow lanes of London laying waste to 13,200 houses, 400 streets as well as devastating the Guildhall and St Paul's Cathedral. Remarkably, though, this instance of domestic disharmony caused the death of just nine people, though the rest were not best pleased at the sights of devastation all around.

Of course, food itself has been the cause of death on many occasions – some of them which make you laugh, even when you shouldn't. There was the nineteenth-century Irish eccentric, Harry Badger, for instance, who could never resist a challenge to eat anything put in front of him. Harry made nothing of drinking dead mice in his beer or eating insects with his meat, but came to a nasty end when he swallowed what was supposed to be a piece of tripe but was actually strips of leather covered in milk.

Then there was the American Robert Pueblo of St Louis who stole a hot dog from a store, crammed it into his mouth before running off, and was found dead a block away with a six-inch piece of the meat lodged in his throat; and the hapless Welshman, Gwilym Connelly, who was stabbed by his wife while she was gesticulating too enthusiastically with a knife as she cut some sandwiches. In this final section, you'll discover that it is not only a good meal that follows in the wake of cooking . . .

The Sucker King

Probably the most famous case of death by food poisoning was that of King John, the youngest son of Henry II, who died in 1216. Legend, however, has made much of this man surnamed Lackland who unsuccessfully tried to seize the crown from his brother, Richard, and not least because of his taste for unusual dishes. According to a biography of his life by Kenneth Norgate written in 1902:

John died of a surfeit of lampreys – an extraordinary eel-like fish with a sucker for a mouth.

The Food Of Love

Raymond de Seillans was a chef who worked for several of the noble families of Provence in France during the closing years of the thirteenth century. When he fell in love with a young lady, he soon found her affections were not for him, but a rising young poet named William de Cabestan. An account of this love triangle is mentioned in a later collection of de Cabestan's verse, which says:

The chef was jealous of his rival and came to him by night and killed him. He cut out the poet's heart and the next day served it up as a special dish to the object of his affections. When the young lady learned the truth of her meal she died of grief.

A Gruelling Fate

Few cooks have suffered a more bizarre fate than Richard Rosse, a well-known London chef in the sixteenth century. In the year 1530, he was appointed to the household of the Bishop of Rochester and appears to have been a good and faithful servant until the autumn. Then, says an account of his life published in *Remarkable Trials & Notorious Characters* (1850):

It was declared that he had poisoned some gruel being made for the Bishop and imprisoned in Smithfield. Here he was boiled to death.

Cold Bacon

The sixteenth-century philosopher and statesman, Francis Bacon, who, it has been suggested, was the man who actually wrote the plays attributed to Shakespeare, was also a dedicated gourmet. In fact, he was constantly searching for ways to improve his cuisine – and one of these killed him, says a biographer, Kuno Fischer, writing in 1827:

On a snow-bound day in March 1626, while out riding with a friend at Highgate, Bacon ordered the coach to be stopped. He had been struck by the thought that snow might be a better preserver of flesh than salt, which was commonly used. Thereupon he purchased a hen from a woman in a nearby cottage, killed it and stuffed the bird with snow. Unfortunately, before he could observe the effect of cold on the preservation of flesh, he took a chill and died.

The Wurst Scenario

German-born Adolph Leutgert was a master butcher in Chicago and determined to make his sausages famous all over the world. In 1874, he did indeed become well known

– but not in the way he had hoped, as a later report in the *Chicago Tribune* states:

> *That year – and for two years afterwards – the sale of sausages in Chicago hit an all-time low. Leutgert, it transpired, had murdered his wife, Louisa, and disposed of her corpse by melting it down in one of his vats and incorporating her into the sausage production line.*

Relative Soup

In the years immediately after the Second World War, many families in Germany were extremely short of food. One such family were the Wallishausers who lived at Hechingen. They managed to sustain themselves thanks to food parcels sent by relatives in America. In March 1946, among the contents of the latest parcel, the family found a can containing an odourless grey powder which they took to be instant soup, says a report in the *National Enquirer*. The story continues:

> *Frau Wallishauser added some semolina to the powder and served it to her family. They all agreed it was the best soup they had tasted since before the war. The following day the Wallishausers received a letter from their relatives in the States. It told them that the little can actually contained the ashes of their grandmother. She had just died – and her last wish had been to be buried in her native soil . . .*

If You Can't Stand The Heat . . .

For thirty years, John Quartero and Joe Cocito, two old friends living in Miami, Florida, met on most nights of the week to share dinner in each other's home. The pair both loved ravioli and Joe Cocito usually made the sauce. One night in September 1958, however, in the middle of a meal, John stood up and walked out. When his friend followed and asked the reason he had left his ravioli unfinished, Quartero whipped a gun from his pocket and shot Cocito in the leg. The *Miami Herald* reported the sad falling out which resulted in Quartero being arrested by Miami police and charged with assault by a deadly weapon. At the police station he explained:

Joe's been making the ravioli sauce hotter and hotter all the time. I just couldn't stand it any longer.

An Injection Of Taste

Vegemite is an Australian spread rather similar to the popular British favourite, Marmite. It featured in a fatal accident to a young man, Paul Maldwyn Cook, of Sydney. A report in the *Sydney Morning Herald* in September 1967 said that the body of the storeman had been found at his home in the Merrylands district of Sydney:

The police state that the 21-year-old man died accidently as a result of injecting himself with Vegemite.

Double Roasting

One Sunday in November 1973, a 55-year-old Parisian, Noel Carriou, was so enraged at being served an over-cooked roast dinner by his wife that he killed her. At his subsequent trial – reported by *Paris-Presse* – it was stated that this was not the first time Carriou's gastronomic juices had boiled over:

Seventeen years ago, M. Carriou, angry at being given undercooked meat, *threw his first wife out of bed so violently that she broke her neck. After seven years in prison, he was released for good conduct and soon married again. After watching a religious programme on television, M. Carriou quarrelled with his second wife about the over-cooked roast. He struck her and she fell and broke her neck. In a plea for leniency, M. Carriou told the jury he believed cooking was the most important duty of a housewife.*

Snails' Pace

Another Frenchman, Marc Quinquandon from Nancy, prided himself on possessing a remarkable appetite and throughout the seventies competed in a number of eating contests. Tragically this pride came before a fatal case of indigestion in 1977. A report of Quinquandon's demise appeared in the local daily paper, *L'Est Republican*:

Quinquandon, a bulldozer driver, became world champion snail-eater 4 months ago by eating 144 snails in eleven and a half minutes. Yesterday, he collapsed during a snail-eating exhibition at a village dance, having just eaten 72 snails in three minutes.

Mobster Meal

Shoichi Murakami was widely feared as one of the most violent gangsters in Tokyo. He was the leader of a gang engaged in a bitter underworld feud with a rival mobster, until his sudden disappearance in the summer of 1978. However, it was not until the autumn of that year that reporters on the *Tokyo Shimbun* were able to piece together what had happened to Murakami. It transpired that he had been ambushed and killed by five gangsters

who then used hatchets to systematically dismember his corpse. The newspaper continued:

> *The larger pieces of the gangster's body were disposed of in the dustbins of a number of Tokyo restaurants. Murakami's hands were cooked so that identification was impossible and then served up in dishes of meat and noodle soups at several street food stalls.*

Cheesed Off With Life

The grocery store run by Luigi Ferrara and his wife in Montmartre, Paris, was well patronised and successful. However, by 1978 the marriage of Luigi and Madame Ferrara was far from all sweetness and light, and climaxed in May when the husband was arrested and charged with murder. The means of death made headlines throughout the nation, for a reason *Le Populaire* explained in one sentence:

> *M. Ferrara has been charged with stabbing his wife to death with a wedge of hard Parmesan cheese.*

A Deadly Banger

On the other side of the world in New Zealand, a not dissimilar case occurred in April 1984. According to the *New Zealand Free Press*, Malcolm Francis of Napier was brought before a court in Wellington accused of murder:

Francis, aged 35, a well-known businessman, has been charged with beating his wife to death with a frozen sausage.

Flame Broiled

In February 1983, the 'Eternal Flame' in Berlin was the subject of an amazing court case when Wolfgang Schurr, an Austrian vagrant, was brought before magistrates. A report in the *Guardian* stated that he had been arrested for heating a saucepan full of onion soup over the flame. The arresting officer told the court:

The 'Eternal Flame' is intended to burn until Germany is reunited and this is Herr Schurr's second offence. Last month he tried to cook a plate of dumplings over the Flame.

Cooked His Goose

In August 1994, 68-year-old Dot Griffiths of Bristol announced that she wanted to be buried with her gas cooker. According to a report in the *Sun* she had made plans for her 1954 New World cooker, 'Belle', to follow her coffin when she was cremated. The paper added:

Dot even threw a 25th birthday party for the stove about which she says, 'The cooker's my true friend.' Husband, Ted, 76, said, 'If it came to a me-or-the-cooker situation, I wouldn't fancy my chances.

Sign From Above

For months, Paolo Ginelli had been looking forward to celebrating his 80th birthday. He had picked the restaurant in Naples where he wanted to dine, selected the menu, and sent out invitations to his large family and many friends. The big night came in November 1994, said a report in *Il Mattino*:

> *The meal was everything that Signor Ginelli had wished for. But as he left the restaurant, a sign fell from the doorway on to his head and killed him.*

Cereal Killer

Police in Munich were initially baffled as to what had killed Pauline Gembach when she was found dead in the family home in April 1995. Later, her husband, Heinrich, was arrested and admitted he had stuffed her to death with food, a report in the *Abend Zeitung* stated. Gembach explained:

> *I forced her to eat lots of wheat cereal. That's what she had given me for breakfast every morning for the last ten years.*

Standing Order

The family of matriarch Carmen Estuanta gathered at the old lady's home in Managua, Nicaragua, in May 1996 for her funeral. There the mourning relatives and friends went about paying their last respects around the coffin of the 100-year-old great-grandmother. But suddenly, ran a report in *La Noticia*, everybody was startled when the 'body' suddenly sat bolt upright. Leon Estuanta, a grandson, filled in the rest of the details:

> *She sat up and asked to be brought some food. The trouble is, this is the third time she has done this to us.*

The Last Word

Despite such culinary catastrophes, wining and dining is still one of the great pleasures, not to say necessities, of human existence. The Chinese – who else – have a succinct yet accurate saying that just fits the bill:

> *How pleasant it is to dine – with nice people.*
> *How pleasant it is to wine – with nice people.*
> *How pleasant it is to sleep [Pause] – with a contended mind.*

THE END – BUT BON APPETITE!